Redcar and Coatham

A HISTORY TO THE END OF THE 19th CENTURY

by

Janet Cockroft

Edited by Peter Sotheran

Line Drawings by M. John Halliwell

First Published December, 1976

PUBLISHER'S NOTE

Chapters 1 to 8 of this work were researched and written by Janet Cockroft. The introduction was written by Peter Sotheran. The line-drawings, except that of Redcar Parish Church, are by M. John Halliwell. All the photographs are from the publisher's library of local historical prints.

Printed and Published by
A. A. SOTHERAN LTD.,
14-16 Queen Street, Redcar, Cleveland

ISBN 0 905032 05 5 (Paper);   0 905032 04 7 (Hardback)

COAT OF ARMS
OF
REDCAR BOROUGH COUNCIL

DESCRIPTION

Barry wavy of six Azure and Argent, a sailing ship proper, pennons flying Gules, in base three fish naiant—two and one—also proper : a chief Sable thereon on a pallet Or, between two steel ingots, a blast furnace, also proper. And for the Crest, on a Wreath of the colours A Lion, rampant and Gules supporting a beacon fired proper.

Motto : Mare et Ferro.

CONTENTS

LIST OF ILLUSTRATIONS

In the Beginning

OUR first picture of life in Britain is drawn for us by Julius Caesar. The ancient Britons who fell to the conquering Romans were hunters who knew nothing of cultivating food. Dressed in skins, they lived in caves or mud huts. They tended to be gregarious, keeping in groups of about a dozen or more, a tribal system. They were fierce, and willing and able to give their all in battle.

With the Romans came civilisation. Sophisticated buildings and organisation supplanted the crude camps of the ancient Britons. In Cleveland the Romans created a line of signal beacons, there was one on Huntcliff and another on top of the Eston Hills. Life for the indigenous natives was still spartan on the coastal plain between the hills and the marshes around the Tees estuary. After nearly five hundred years of generally good government the Romans withdrew to defend territories nearer to Rome. Unused to liberty and totally unprepared to rule themselves the Britons found themselves in a predicament. The marauding Picts and Scots, finding no Romans defending the wall built to keep them out, were able to overrun the country in the north.

Defenceless, after five centuries of Roman protection, the Britons begged the Saxons to help restore order. Hengist and Horsa, sons of a famous Saxon general came to Britain in AD 449. Three years later the whole of the lands north of the Humber were in the hands of the Saxons. The Britons were driven from their own lands, those who remained were slaves to the Saxons. Although brave and daring fighters, the Saxons at peace were industrious. They tilled the land, kept cattle and lived in permanent settlements. They also brought with them their language, customs and place names. One group settled in the middle of the plain, halfway between Huntcliff and the mouth of the Tees. They called it Mersc after the marshes which covered much of the ground. Popular custom has it that Redcar takes its name from the reeds of the marshes and the scars of rock on the shore. Over the last 800 years the place has been called "Riedcarre," "Ridekarre," "Reddkerr," "Redcarre," and by 1790, Redcar.

Christianity established under the Romans in 324 AD was banished by the Saxons who placed their faith in Woden. The days of the week which we use today are corruptions of the Saxon gods. Having established themselves, the country existed in comparative peace for two centuries.

A political marriage helped the return of Christianity to the north. To strengthen his position as ruler of Bernica, the land between the Tees and the Forth, Edwin, son of Aella, sought to marry Ethelberga, daughter of Ethelbert, King of Kent. Both king and daughter had been converted to Christianity by the missionary Augustine. The marriage was arranged, conditional on the woman and her attendants being allowed freedom of worship. The monk Paulinus joined the ruler's household as chaplain, and two years later Edwin was converted. He was baptised on Easter Day, 627, in a wooden chapel located where York Minster now stands. Many other nobles turned to Christianity too, among them his niece, Hilda, later to be Abbess of Whitby. A decade later, Saint Aidan, from Iona, came to the area. Monasteries were founded at Whitby and Hartlepool.

A further two centuries passed and the Viking invaders came in force. Christianity was again banished. Settlements were uprooted and the people driven into the hills. Bloodshed, ravaging and an unsettled way of life returned.

Peace returned under the reign of Athelstan. Christianity was again encouraged and the work was furthered by Dunstan and Edward the Confessor, 1042-66. William the Conqueror came, and after reigning less than a year, Harold II, went. Three years after the Battle of Hastings, the Normans were still at work subduing the Anglo-Saxons. The last resistance came from Edgar the Atheling and a group of northern chiefs which included Gospatric, ancestor of the Marquess of Zetland. The last battle was fought on the marshes at Coatham; the defensive earthworks remained visible until early this century. They are now lost beneath the iron and steel complexes. The Normans won the day and in retaliation put the north of England to the sword and the flame. The Domesday Book records many places as *terrae wastae*—waste lands.

AFTER THE CONQUEST

GEOLOGISTS tell us that forty thousand years ago, a huge forest covered the area from Hartlepool to Whitby. Before the Glacial period, when the seas rose, it stretched for many miles out into the North Sea. The Tees probably entered the sea south of its present estuary, somewhere near Marske. Many wild and strange animals roamed the area. After the Conquest, a Grant, dated 25th May, 1280, was made to Lord Walter De Faucenberg, allowing him a free warren to hunt wild boar, deer, wolf and elk "inn ye forests off Reidkarre".

An ancient market was organised for Redcar as early as 1257. Marmaduke de Thweng procured a King's licence for a market and fair, and although King Edward confirmed the Charter in 1293, there are no records showing the success or failure of the venture. The saltworks at Coatham had existed for some six hundred years by this time.

AN ANCIENT CHURCH

COPSI, an uncle of Harry Hotspur, the infamous Earl of Northumberland, gave fifty acres of land at "Reidkarre" to St. Cuthbert's Church, Durham. A century later, Ivo de Grancestre gave the Prior of Guisborough a portion of land at Redcar on which to build a chapel. No precise records remain, but this was, almost without doubt, the ancient Sepulchre Chapel, which stood for five or six centuries from the mid-twelfth century, amongst the sandbanks at Coatham.

Much research was done into the history of the old chapel by Thomas McAll Fallow, M.A., F.S.A., who retired to Coatham in 1872 and was an active member of the parish church and served on several public bodies. The chapel probably stood near to Marsh House Farm, in the shadow of the Redcar Steel Complex. Mrs. Faith, who had lived at the farm as a child in the first half of the nineteenth century, knew of the chapel and remembered seeing the remains of the walls near the farm. Stones were removed from the walls to repair outbuildings of the farmhouse. A Mr. Suggett remembered finding several skulls and other remains while digging in the vicinity of the chapel site, at the same period as Mrs. Faith. A prominent sandhill, immediately north-east of the farm was known as "Church Hill" from its proximity to the chapel.

After the gift of the land by Ivo de Grancestre in 1150, three centuries elapsed before the next written reference to the chapel. This occurred in the will of Robert Taylor of East Coatham, dated 5th October, 1470; twelve pence (5p) was bequeathed towards the repair of the chapel of Saint Sulpitius. Another man of East Coatham made his will on 10th December, 1473. In it he bequeathed his soul "to God the Father Almighty, to Blessed Mary, and to all the Saints," and directed that his body be buried within the chapel of Saint Sulpitius in the parish of Kirkleatham, which at that time, of course extended to the sea. He went on to endow the living with the income from rents of various specified lands and tenements in Kirkleatham, Upleatham and Seaton Carew; this endowment was conditional on the inhabitants obtaining a Royal Licence which would enable the chapel to become parochial in its own right. Since Coatham remained a part of Kirkleatham Parish until the nineteenth century we can assume that it was a dream never realised. William Raughton (or Raughtonbald) in his will around 1500, left to "Saint Syplyn A nawter clothe and a Kandylstik"—an altar cloth and candlestick; this testament was written in English.

Nothing is to be discovered about the chapel for half a century. In 1545 an Act of Parliament was passed empowering Henry VIII to dissolve the many religious establishments throughout the country and seize their property; the proceeds were to defray the costs of the French and Scottish wars. Commissioners were employed to enquire into the nature and purpose of the churches and to prepare inventories of their property and income. The Commissioners for Yorkshire presented the following report, dated 14th February, 1547:

> "The Chapell called Sepulchres Chapell in the Paryshe of Kyrkelethome. William Arnarde Incumbent there of thaige fforty yeres of honeste conversacion and qualities and of good lerneninge, having no other promocions but only the revenewe of the said chauntery or chapel. The necessitie of the said chapell is to do divine service to the inhabitaunts there, being distaunt frome the parishe churche twoo myles, and there is in the said parishe of howselling people (communicants) to the number of cccxii., and there is no landes ne tenements sold sithens the said xxiii. day of November in the year of the reign of the late King Henry VIII the thirty-seventh (1546). "The yerely value of said chapell is as shall appere by the particulars of sayme, xlvij s. iiij d. (£2.36) Summa of the said chapel xlvij s. iiij d. which remain."

In 1575, Queen Elizabeth I issued a Commission of Inquiry into certain "concealed lands", as they were called, in Yorkshire. Of Kirkleatham, the Commissioners reported the following:

> "And also that there is a free chapel with appurtenances and a yard belonging to it in the parish of Kirkleadam, otherwise

called Seplyns Chapell, in the said County of York, the land containing by estimation one acre more or less, now or lately in the tenure or occupation of Christopher Marshall or his assigns. And also that there are twelve swathes of grass in Este and Weste Coatham Inges in Cleveland . . . and appropriated for one priest called the Chauntrie Priest (of) the Chapel of Seplyns."

East and West Coatham Ings were land around Marsh House Farm, particularly to the south and west of it. It is likely that the farm house is on the site of, and may comprise parts of, the residence of these early chaplains at Coatham.

The next reference to the chapel is in the thirteenth year of Elizabeth I (1578) when an indenture was enrolled in chancery by which Edmund Downynge and Milo Doddinge, both notorious land jobbers of London, sold to Richard Bellasis of Morton, Durham, all "le frontland" containing half an acre, and the arable lands at Kirkleatham which had belonged to the late Chantry of "St. Sulphon". Frontland or frontstead was a term applied to a site on which a house or other building stood. From the Bellasis family, the manor of Kirkleatham with this piece of church property passed by purchase to John Turner of Guisborough. More of the Turners and their successors presently.

In a conveyance dated 9th July, 1632, Robert Coulthirst (whose fine memorial brass is still in Kirkleatham church) assigned to John Turner some lands in East Coatham, including "one parcel of ground called . . . Kirkhill . . . adjoining East Coatham coney warren". The Church Hill was levelled and removed around the time that the railway reached Redcar in the early 1800's.

Five variations of name were given to the chapel; St. Sulpitius, St. Seplyn, St. Sulphon, Sepulchre's, St. Cyprian. An early correspondent wrote (Cotton Manuscripts, British Museum):

"They have a tradycion that the Danes used to land there (at Dabholm, as Coatham was then called) showing great heapes of bones in the sands . . . whether they had got a crust or noe, or that there were some charnell house there I know not, wch I suspecte by a reason that a chapell . . . is neare at hand."

The allusion to a charnell house in connection with the chapel is interesting and instructive in that it affords a clue to the origin of the name of Sepulchre's Chapel. St. Seplyn's and St. Sulphon are manifest errors on the part of some copyist. In interpreting place names, the oldest form usually gives the best clue to the origin. Sulpitius was the earliest, and is a quite reasonable dedication for a chapel; a chapel at York Minster bore the same dedication before the Reformation. The Coatham chapel may well have served as a burial place for sailors washed up on the beaches and thus become known as the Sepulchre Chapel. St. Sulphon was probably a contraction of Sulpitius. St. Cyprian was probably a conjectured correction of Seplyn.

The building itself was probably small and without any architectural distinction. Being Norman, the windows would have rounded or slightly pointed heads. It is doubtful if there was anything to divide the sanctuary from the nave of the church. There would be a bell gable at the west end. From the bequests for repairs in the fifteenth century, it is apparent that there was work to be done; the building was very likely altered somewhat to the perpendicular style of that century.

KIRKLEATHAM

KIRKLEATHAM takes its name from an Anglo-Saxon word "hlipum" meaning a slope. The "Kirk" prefix was added and subtracted through the centuries to distinguish the village from Upleatham.

Of Kirkleatham, the Domesday Book records that there were nine carucates of land and five ploughs. Uctred had a manor there but following the Conquest it was given to Earl Morton, having been laid waste in the Harrying of the North. In King Edward's time, the land had been worth 16 shillings but after the devastation is was reduced to 5 shillings and 4 pence. There was a priest and a church.

Robert de Brus was granted Kirkleatham along with about 180 other manors in the north, for his part in the Conquest. Thence it passed to Marmaduke de Thweng who lived at Kilton Castle near Brotton. Through the marriage of Lucy, eldest sister of Thomas de Thweng, Kirkleatham came into the hands of the Lumleys. As a result of crimes against the State, it was forfeited to the Crown. Queen Elizabeth I granted it to Sir William Bellasis, knight. He in turn conveyed the estate to John Turner Esquire in 1623. It stayed in the hands of the Turners until Sir Charles Turner willed it to his widow, who married Henry Vansittart Esquire in 1812.

Their daughter, Teresa Vansittart married her cousin, Lieut. Arthur Newcomen, R.H.A., in 1841. They had two daughters, Alice Teresa and Eveleen, and two sons, Charles Montgomerie and Arthur Henry Turner, who was heir to the estates. Teresa Newcomen (née Vansittart) applied much of her wealth to the founding of Coatham Parish Church and the Convalescent Home. Arthur H. T. Newcomen never inherited the estates, dying before his mother; on her death, the property passed to Arthur's son, Gleadhowe. Gleadhowe never married and at his death, Kathleen Teresa Turner Newcomen succeeded to the estate in 1932. Kathleen had married Colonel Le Roy Lewis and they had one son and four daughters. On the death of Mrs. Le Roy Lewis, the estate passed to the son, Henry. The following year, 1949, he sold the house to Ortem Estates and the land to another company. The hospital eventually passed through the hands of the Charity Commissioners to a Board of Trustees.

CHAPTER ONE — 1800 - 1820

A T the beginning of the nineteenth century, Redcar and Coatham were two quite separate villages a mile apart. Coatham was in the parish of Kirkleatham, Redcar was mainly in the parish of Marske although a small portion of the village belonged to the parish of Upleatham.

Upleatham controlled a square portion on the foreshore at the east end of the village. How this came about is not absolutely clear, it seems likely that the manor at Upleatham held certain fishing rights at Redcar and that these were secured by the attachment of the land to Upleatham parish. The boundary between the parishes of Marske and Kirkleatham ran along the present West Dyke road.

Coatham was part of the Kirkleatham Estate and, as such, it belonged to the Turner family at Kirkleatham Hall who had purchased it in 1623. Redcar was part of the Marske Estate, owned by the Dundas family, having been purchased by Sir Lawrence Dundas in 1762. His grandson also called Lawrence was created Earl of Zetland in 1838 and the title is perpetuated by the family who still maintain many interests around Marske-by-Sea and live at Aske, near Richmond, Yorkshire.

The first national census was taken in 1801. Redcar is recorded as consisting of 115 inhabited houses containing 125 families. There were 170 males and 261 females. That the females greatly outnumbered the males could be partially explained by the fact that as many of the men were seafarers there was always a great number away from home.

This first census included Coatham with the rest of the parish of Kirkleatham. The population of the whole parish was 680 living in 159 houses. The population of Coatham would be about half of this, or a little less.

TOTAL POPULATION FIGURES

Census	Redcar	Kirkleatham
1801	431	680
1811	411	622
1821	673	686

The population of Redcar decreased during the first decade of the century for no particular reason then, in the following decade it increased by 50 per cent. Kirkleatham also suffered a decrease but later recovered its losses although without a dramatic increase as at Redcar. Coincidental with the lower census returns, Europe was in the throes of the Napoleonic Wars. It is feasible that many seafaring men were involved in the navy. As Redcar continued to grow as a resort, Kirkleatham's population remained almost static for the following forty years.

In his book *The History of Cleveland*, published in 1808, Revd. Graves described Redcar as "a considerable fishing town situated close upon the beach". He adds that Redcar "consisted formerly of a few miserable huts only, inhabited by fishermen and their families; but is now a place of fashionable resort for sea-bathing." Redcar was visited during the summer months by genteel families from the surrounding countryside. The number of lodging houses increased each year and Graves found them to be "neat and commodious". As a visitor to the town, he was surprised to see heaps of drift sand nearly as high as the cottages!

Coatham was similar, though quieter, and in Graves' opinion— superior, more suited to cater for invalids seeking the bracing sea air than was Redcar which he rated as a poorer community. Graves also came upon "a large and commodious inn". The was the Lobster Inn, built some years earlier by Charles Turner who had done much to improve the amenities and roads of the area. Graves seems to have enjoyed his stay in the two resorts as he praised their gentility and simplicity. Indeed he wished that the "innocent enjoyments of Coatham might be found in other watering places instead of the passion for gambling."

In 1810 was published Hutton's celebrated *A Trip to Coatham.* W. Hutton journeyed to Coatham from Birmingham at the age of 86, with his invalid daughter who, he hoped, would benefit from the sea air. A distinguished antiquarian, he took a great interest in Redcar and Coatham, declaring, "I shall have the honour of being their first historian".

He described Redcar and Coatham as two hamlets which "an age back could have been no more than small fishing places, which, instead of being known one hundred miles off, were scarcely known by their neighbours". They were in fact two small villages separated by an open green. Coatham was a single street built along the south side only; Hutton estimates that there were around seventy houses. Redcar was also a single street, built on both north and south sides and consisted of one hundred and fifteen houses.

The mountains of drift sand covering the streets were still a feature of the villages and made walking difficult. Hutton jokes "no carriage above a wheelbarrow ought to venture". In some places the sandbanks came right up to the eaves of the cottages and doorways needed clearing each day. A century ahead of the event, Hutton approved the principle of an amalgam of the two neighbouring villages, believing that it would benefit both places. Times were untroubled. There was no constable stationed in the fishing villages and according to Hutton, there was no need for one. The people were clean and well-mannered and the children well-kept. He did not see a single "ragged person".

The sea was the mainstay of life for many. Coatham had about a dozen cobles and Redcar twenty-eight. As well as fish the sea yielded sea-coal, both were used by the locals themselves and also resold. From the twentieth century we must wonder at the panorama of the seascape with upwards of fifty sailing ships passing between Hartlepool and Huntcliff each day.

Both Redcar and Coatham were quiet watering places. Amusements were simple. Visitors were content with the beach and bracing air during the day and a game of cards at night. No doubt they also took outings to the pleasant unspoilt villages in the neighbourhood. The roads were remarkably fine for the time, suitable for walking, riding, or travelling by carriage. The sea was the main attraction. Excursion parties would take to the sea for three or four hours, sailing down to Saltburn and back, or across the bay to Seaton where they might disembark for tea before returning. There was also a lending library and for a few years a small theatre. As the century progressed local entrepreneurs catered more and more for the visitors. Bicycles, tricycles and baby-carriages could be hired by the hour or day. By prior arrangement, the guest-houses would have a pianoforte installed for your amusement.

The sea-bathing was what the visitors really sought. Coatham had four bathing machines and Redcar a dozen. Public bathing was still a new idea and had yet to be approved of in higher social circles. The sparsity of bathing machines at Coatham was in keeping with its image as the more socially acceptable of the two resorts. The price of a 'dip' from a bathing machine was around one shilling. There were also facilities for warm water bathing, rather expensive at three shillings and sixpence a time. Compare those charges with the cost of lodgings. A family could rent a suite of rooms or a whole house for between two and five guineas per week. Hutton detailed the expenses for himself and his invalid daughter when they stayed at the Public Hotel.

For each person	.	.	.	.	4s. 6d.
For the coachman	.	.	.	.	3s.
For each of the two horses	.	.	.	3s.

PLAN OF REDCAR 1815

AT this time Redcar consisted of one street—the High Street— and comprised one hundred and fifteen houses and three inns. On the south side there were sixty-two houses, most of which had long gardens behind them. The fishermen would keep a few hens, perhaps a pig and grow a few vegetables. Many houses are shown with small outbuildings at the end of the plots. These were the bait-houses where the fishing tackle was kept and prepared. Some of these little buildings still survive amongst the commercial property backing on to Lord Street. There was also the Red Lion Inn, an old-established inn with stables immediately behind it, across Lord Street. On the North side there were forty-eight houses, some of which had long gardens running down to the beach. The other two inns were on this side, the Swan and the Ship Inn. Five more houses stood in the middle of the thoroughfare. Along the sea front were the gardens, yards and offices of the High Street traders. The only building was the lifeboat house.

At the western end of the village was the first Zetland School, built in 1807. The school, with a house for the master, was built and endowed by Sir Lawrence Dundas, first Earl of Zetland, who lived at Upleatham Hall. The master was to teach ten children free of charge and was restricted to a charge of not more than four shillings a quarter for the instruction of the children of pilots and labourers. The old school was used for fifty years until the present Zetland School was built, near Redcar Parish Church. It stood in what is now West Terrace, on a site presently occupied by the office of an Estate Agent. Next to the school stood the Methodist Meeting House. This was the first place of worship in Redcar and remained the only one until the building of St. Peter's Parish Church in 1829. From Hutton's comments we learn that the Methodist Meetings were always well attended.

In 1815 there were two bath houses, very necessary in those days before the advent of sanitation and concern for personal hygiene amongst the 'working classes'. One establishment was run by Mr.

19

Carter; the other being Stamps's baths. Their positions are indicated on the Plan of 1815. Later there were to be Spence's and Skinner's Baths. The latter was established by the grandfather of Charles Skinner who was known by two generations of Redcar youngsters as he ran the Model Shop in Station Road and latterly on the Esplanade. Skinner's baths were on Lord Street opposite the Police Station. Mr. Spence's establishment was between Cleveland Street and the Esplanade.

The Poor House consisted of two cottages, which as the name tells, were used 'for the reception of the poor'. This was prior to the building of the Workhouse at Guisborough. This latter establishment became part of Guisborough General Hospital.

At this time, Redcar was part of the ecclesiastical parish of Marske. The old church of St. Germain was the parish church and was usually reached by the cliff-top paths or by carriage, via Redcar Lane and Redcar Road at Marske; at times of low water, the direct route was on to the beach at Granville Terrace, Redcar and up Spout Chine (the Valley Gardens) at Marske. A parish hearse was provided for funerals of people from Redcar. It was kept in the Hearse House, situated at the rear of 151 and 153 High Street. Parts of this property survive today virtually unchanged.

The rules for the use of the Parish Hearse stipulated that it was not to travel more than twenty miles from Redcar and that the innkeeper who took it away was responsible for it and for collecting the hire fares. The hearse was bought by public subscription in 1812 and 102 people contributed to its cost. Subscribers could expect one free journey, others paid as follows: Stokesley 10s. 6d., Guisborough and Ormesby 6s., Wilton 4s., Skelton 5s., Kirkleatham 3s. 6d. Between Redcar and Marske the 'fare' was 2s. 6d., Coatham to Marske 3s. 6d.

One name which appears on the list of householders accompanying the old town plan is that of Fleck. James Fleck married Margaret, sister of Captain James Cook, R.N., the circumnavigator. Margaret had been living at Redcar, with her father, also a James Cook, at the time. Captain Cook was killed in Hawaii, February 14th, 1779. His father, a day labourer, died at Redcar on April 1st of the same year. Margaret, wife of James Fleck, died on 9th August, 1798, aged 26 years. Her husband, a master mariner like her brother, died April 20th, 1828, aged 64. Several of the family, including Captain Cook's father, are buried in St. Germain's churchyard at Marske.

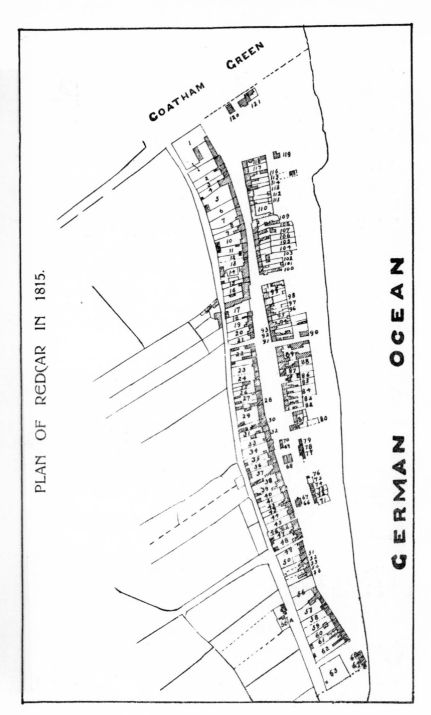

PLAN OF REDCAR IN 1815.

COATHAM GREEN

GERMAN OCEAN

KEY TO THE PLAN OF REDCAR

HOUSES, Etc., ON SOUTH SIDE

Note: H—House; G—Garden

1 Messrs. Foster and Duck, H. G. &c.
2 Zachariah Gardener, H & G
3 Mary Boagy, H and G
4 Thomas Rudd, H and G
5 Robert Henderson, H.
6 Widow Pignette, H and G
7 Tho. Mill, H and G
8 Mary Davison, H and Yard
9 James Henderson, H and G
10 Wm. Clement, H and G and Stackyard
11 Joseph Dove, H and G
12 Ann Allan, H and G
13 Robert Simpson, H and G
14 Messrs. Foster and Duck, H, G, &c.
15 Ralph Greensides, H and G
16 Mrs. Carlton, Inn and Offices
17 Joseph Fenwick, Barn and Garth
18 Tho. Thompson, H & G
19 { Dorothy Andrew, H and G
   { Geo. Robinson, H & G
20 Elizabeth Walton, H and Garth
21 Robert Barker, H and G
22 Wm. Smith, H and G
23 Tho. Burnegal, H and G
24 Tho. Burnegal, H and G
25 Wm. Marfleet, H and G
26 Margt. Potts, H and G
27 Margaret Dowton, H and G
28 Margt. Wilson, H and G
29 Mrs. Law, H and G
30 Wm. Johnson, H and G
31 Slater Potts, H and G
32 John Dobson, senr., H and G
33 John Dobson, senr., H and G
34 William Potts, H and G
35 William Bladderwick
36 Tho. Hall, H and G
37 Jonathan Milner, H and G
38 William Webster, H and G
39 Rev. Mr. Saul, H and G
40 James Lynas, H and G
41 Thos. Thompson, H and G
42 Peter Walton, H and G
43 Tho. Thompson, H and G
44 Wm. Thompson, H and G
45 Wm. Guy, H and G
46 Dorothy Potts, H and G
47 William Johnson, H and G
48 John Busby, H and G
49 Palister Thompson, H and G
50 John Carlton, H and G
51 John Spurr, H and G
52 Mary Watson, H and G
53 Robert Burnegal, H and G
54 William Bladderwick
55 James Fleck, H and G
56 Tho. Agar, H, Garth, &c.
56a John Trattles, H and G
57 John Eden, H and G
58 Tho. Robson, H and G
59 Simpson Adamson, H and G
60 Mrs. Agar, H and G
61 John Brown, H and G
62 Rev. Jos. Smith, H and G
63 Richard Dobson, G

64 Richard Dobson, H
65 Richard Dobson, H
66 Chr. Robinson, H
67 John Crane, H
68 Jonathan Milner, H and G } In the middle of the Street
69 Thos. Hall, H
70 William Potts, H

HOUSES Etc. ON NORTH SIDE

71 Josh. Pounder, H and G
72 Tho. Hall, H and G
73 James Fleck, H and G
74 Poor Houses
75 The Pinfold
76 The Hearse House
77 Mary Graham, H
78 Mary Carlton, H
79 Tho. Robinson, H
80 John Hutton, H and G
81 { Robt. Boagy, H and Yard
   { John Dobson, jun. H and Yard
   { Tho. Bilton, H and Yard
82 Ralph Greensides, H and G
83 Mr. Bell, H and G
84 Margt. Wilson, 2 Houses & Offices
85 Thos. Fleck, H and G
86 Mary Davison, H and G
87 Malcolm McNaughton, H and G
88 Tho. Thompson, H and G
89 John Eden, Inn, House & Offices
90 Lifeboat House
91 Geo. Johnson, H. Offices &c.
92 Chr. Moor, H. and Offices
93 Tho. Walton, H etc.
94 John Walton, H etc.
95 Margt. Waistal, H etc.
96 Saml. Richley, H etc.
97 Ralph Carter, H etc.
98 John Richley, H etc.
99 Jas. Carter, 2 Houses & Offices
100 Jas. Carter, H, Baths, &c.
101 William Smith, H and Offices
102 Eliz. Clarke, House etc.
103 Thos. Potts, H and G
104 W. Webster, H and G
105 Joseph Dove, H and G
106 Alice Potts, H etc.
107 John Thwaites, H etc.
108 Esther Darnton, H etc.
109 Joseph Barnett, H and G
110 Mrs. Carlton, 2 Houses and G
111 James Lynas, H and Offices
112 Ann Winn, H and Office
113 Ann Stamp, H etc.
114 Mr. Horner, H etc.
115 John Barnett, H etc.
116 John Spurr, H and G
117 John Wilkinson, H etc.
118 Mary Hull, H etc.
119 Geo. Stamp, Baths
120 Soc. of Methodists' Meeting House
121 School House and Yard

Part of Upleatham

THE BUILDINGS

ONE or two of the oldest cottages were cruck built. The main structure of the building was carried by huge 'A' frames, usually either three, or five in larger buildings which would also accommodate some livestock. The frames were erected in a row, forming a tent-like structure. With the tops linked to form the ridge, the crossbars were joined and crude walls of local materials—rocks, stones, or clay filled in up to the level of the crossbars, usually six or seven feet above the ground. The earliest of the dwellings were thatched. As the eighteenth century turned into the nineteenth, red tiles predominated.

The smaller cruck houses had a central passageway from the entrance, at right angles to the length of the building; one side would be living quarters, the other work space or sleeping quarters. In later years, the cross-members of the frames were boarded across to make a loft, either for storage or sleeping. The longer, five cruck, houses would be divided roughly into one-third and two-thirds. The smaller portion was the living quarters and was separated from the larger end by a passage-way which crossed the house from wall to wall with entrances at either side. These larger buildings predominated in rural areas and the larger portion accommodated the smallholder's livestock. Before lofts were made, smoke from a central hearth escaped through a smoke hole or the eaves; later chimneys were incorporated.

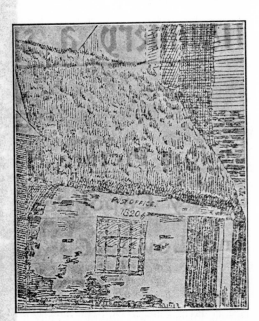

Redcar's original post office functioned for some years, from around 1820 in a cruck house. It was located between the Red Lion Inn and the west end of the High Street. The last of the ancient cruck houses in Redcar was demolished in 1911. "Old Pott's Cottage" as it was known, stood at 118 High Street where there is now a solicitor's office. This cottage was recorded in a census taken during the reign of Henry VIII (1509-1547). When it was demolished, a smuggler's 'dark cupboard' or gin-cupboard was discovered.

The overall appearance of the cottages was one of cleanliness and good order. In front of many, on their seaward side, were low buildings which served dual purposes as outhouses and as barriers to the wind-blown sand. These have long since vanished but there are still a number in Coatham.

THE YEOMAN'S HOUSE, COATHAM

BUILT in 1698, and standing in Coatham High Street, it is the oldest surviving house in the town and one of the oldest in Cleveland. Along with the date of its construction, the builder placed above the door the initials of the man and woman who first owned the house. The original house is now divided into two dwellings. The real front door was that under the engraved lintel. A small oval window nearby was the "fire window" which allowed light on to the hearth, which was otherwise in considerable shadow because of the large smoke hood. The original stone mullions make the other windows worthy of interest also.

REDCAR HIGH STREET

A NUMBER of handsome middle-class houses were built along the High Street during the later years of the eighteenth century. A good example is number 44, now part of Boots shop, which was built in 1772. Another building well preserved above its commercial frontage is that of Greenwood's Menswear at number 47, built in 1778. Probably the oldest building is 98 High Street, now occupied by an insurance company. It is a neat three storeyed house, thought to have been built in the seventeenth century. At the side of the property is a narrow passage leading to Lord Street.

Several large buildings, now public houses, were the superior homes of the eighteenth century. The Stockton Hotel was built before 1703 and at that time was owned by Mrs. Mary Hall and Ann Blatherwick as their dwelling. The "Crown and Anchor" was demolished and rebuilt about 1967. Its predecessor with the same name was built as a private house in 1778. Regulars at the old "Crown and Anchor" remember with affection the tiny rooms, the cosy fireplaces and the narrow passages through the building.

The oldest document referring to the Red Lion Inn is dated 1761. Occupied by John Skirton, farmer, it was almost certainly a farmhouse. By the beginning of the nineteenth century it was a popular inn. The age of the building is readily discerned from the

Coatham Marshes, 1976

Plate 1

Marsh House Farm, Warrenby, 1926

Esplanade, 1890

Plate 2

High Street, 1875 (opposite) Plate 3

THE REDCAR OLD LIFEBOAT, "ZETLAND."

T. H. NELSON, Photo.

Plate 4

rear access. In the cobbled yard are a mounting block and stables. Extensive stables adjacent to the rear of the hotel, across Lord Street were used as a riding school during this century until their closure, prior to demolition in the 1970s. The Swan Hotel, previously an inn, can also be traced back to the eighteenth century.

One of the finest remaining buildings of the early nineteenth century is 151 High Street. It is again a three storeyed house with original sash windows and a pilastered doorway. One distinctive style occurring in many buildings of this period is the long window with a semi-circular head over the landing halfway up the stairs. These are still obvious at the rear of 143, 145, 151 High Street and several others nearby.

THE PORT OF COATHAM

DURING the first decade of the nineteenth century, Coatham was still a small port and it belonged to the Kirkleatham Estate. In 1778, Charles Turner appointed John Agar, a yeoman of Coatham, "to collect the duties of anchorage, groundage and beaconage". Between 1789 and 1808 John Agar kept a record of the movement of the ships and the monies he collected. (The note book is preserved at the North Riding County Record Office). Many of the ships putting in to Coatham were from Sunderland, Hartlepool, Stockton and Whitby. Their cargoes were mainly coal, lime and building materials; they unloaded at the water's edge and the goods were hauled across the sands. Other vessels anchored off Coatham to await a favourable wind to carry them up the Tees to the ports of Yarm or Stockton and later to Middlesbrough.

In 1808 the Tees Navigation Company was created by Act of Parliament and thus the Turner family lost rights to the shipping dues. The Tees was about to become a major port. At the time the Navigation Company was founded, Middlesbrough was still a farm with a derelict priory; Newport, Linthorpe and Acklam were separate villages. With the development of Stockton's port in 1825, Yarm declined. When the railways arrived in Middlesbrough three years later, trade again moved down the river. The earliest coal staithes were at Port Clarence in 1833 and Port Darlington, adjacent to the end of what is now Linthorpe Road in 1830. The development of the coal and later the iron industries needed these more efficient port facilities, consequently, the port of Coatham declined very rapidly.

THE " ZETLAND " LIFEBOAT

THE oldest surviving lifeboat in the world is preserved in Redcar. She was built at South Shields in 1800 by Henry Greathead and originally stationed at Spurn Point in the Humber Estuary. However, she did not see much active service and was offered for sale. The fishermen of Redcar bought her for £100 and named her "Zetland". The boathouse was given by Lord Zetland and was situated close to the beach on the site of the present lifeboat station.

When the boat was called out, a boy was sent round the town beating a drum to summon the crew. Men and women would strain together to wheel the boat across the beach to the sea. Later a rocket maroon was used to call out the crew and the boat hauled by horses in to the water. A specially trained team of eight horses were kept at Ings Farm. On hearing the rocket's explosion, the farmer released the horses and they galloped down Redcar Lane on their own, often arriving before the crew. The "Zetland" arrived at Redcar in 1802. Between then and her final withdrawal from service in 1880, she saved over 500 lives.

CHAPTER TWO — 1820 - 1840

THE 1820's were to find Redcar growing in popularity as a sea-bathing resort. At the same time its fishing activities were flourishing. The market for Redcar fish extended inland beyond the immediately neighbouring communities.

Baine's Yorkshire, one of the earliest directories was compiled in 1823. The information in the directory reflects the growing importance of Redcar. One is struck by the number of shopkeepers and craftsmen in the village. As well as several grocers, drapers and shoemakers, there were jewellers, milliners, a hairdresser and even a straw-bonnet maker. Alongside their main trade, many shops dealt in a wide range of other goods; it would seem curious today to find a shoemaker who was also a tea dealer. Five inns were listed in the directory, the "Jolly Sailor" and the "Crown and Anchor" being the recent additions. There were twenty-five lodging house keepers and many other people took in paying guests during the season. It is also recorded that a few gentlefolk had found a quiet retreat in Redcar, or taken up residence to benefit from the clean, bracing air. Redcar was clearly thriving.

The rival resort of Coatham, a mile away, was losing popularity as a resort by the 1820's. In his *Dictionary of Towns, Hamlets and Villages of Yorkshire,* Thomas Langdale comments, "Few people now resort to Coatham for bathing because it is further from the sea than Redcar". Bain's directory does not record any lodging houses and still only one inn. We conclude that with the demise of its port, Coatham had remained a small hamlet and was reverting to its agricultural living.

Visitors to the area travelled by coach or carriage. During the season, a coach ran three times a week from Bedale. It travelled via Northallerton, Stokesley and Guisborough and was known as "The Cleveland". Alternate journeys the coach rested at the Red Lion and Swan inns. From Northallerton there was a connection with the Leeds coach.

Besides the old Zetland school in West Terrace, there was a small private school, or "Academy" as it styled itself. At Coatham there was a small free school "for the education of fifty poor children". This school had been established by the Turner family of Kirkleatham Hall, in 1811. Twelve of the children were given a suit of clothes each year.

ST. PETER'S CHURCH

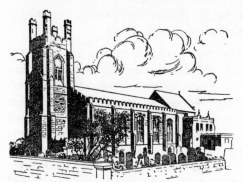

DESPITE Redcar's growing importance and rising population, the only place of worship was the Methodist Chapel. Church of England members were expected to attend the old church of St. Germain at Marske. For hundreds of years, funeral processions from Redcar had walked three miles along the beach to Marske. The coffin was carried by bearers, the mourners singing hymns as they walked behind. The cortège would wind its way up from the beach by the "Corpse Path". The coffin would be set down by the wayside cross on the edge of the Headlands opposite Cliff House at Marske for a while. When the bearers were rested the procession would move slowly along the last half-mile of cliff-top path to St. Germain's Church. The alternative route was via Redcar Lane in the Parish Hearse.

In 1821 St. Germain's was in a dilapidated state and was demolished and rebuilt but could no longer accommodate the many summer visitors. In 1823, a petition was sent to the Justices of the Peace at Northallerton stating :

> "That the inhabitants of Redcar who, together with those of the adjoining village of Coatham, amount to one thousand souls, exclusive of five hundred visitors who resort there during the bathing season, are desirous of attending public worship . . . but are unable to do so from the impossibility of accommodation in the parish church, and on account of its great distance."

Later that year, the foundation stone of St. Peter's Church was laid. However, funds were not sufficient for its completion for a further six years. It was consecrated by the Archbishop of York in 1829. The church has been described as a standing monument to the benevolence of the Zetland family. The Earl of Zetland gave the land for the site, the stone for the building and a handsome donation besides. The Church Building Society contributed £500 and the balance was raised by public subscription.

St. Peter's Parish Church is a plain stone building with a small tower. The turrets on the tower are a useful landmark for local fishermen, guiding them through the Saltscar rocks. Inside, the original building was typical of its time, being furnished with box pews (removed in 1888). The original seating accommodated seven hundred people; four hundred and eighty seats were free, the remainder were rented to the wealthier families. Within twenty years the continuing growth of the town necessitated extensions to the building. The first priest-in-charge was the vicar of Upleatham; he travelled between his churches on a donkey.

The communities of Redcar and Marske would have been much the poorer without the generous provisions of the Zetlands. The original village school on West Terrace had been provided by Lawrence Dundas, Earl of Zetland; other buildings included the lifeboat house, the present Zetland School adjacent to St. Peter's church. At Marske the family provided two schools, St. Mark's Parish Church and the Village Institute. In this century the present Marquis of Zetland presented Marske Hall to the Leonard Cheshire Foundation Homes for Sick.

THE WRECK OF THE " ESK "

THE Yorkshire coast is a dangerous one in times of gales and storms. There is no readily accessible refuge harbour between the Humber and the Tyne. Entering Whitby was impossible when running before a storm in a sailing ship. The rocks at Redcar claimed many boats and countless lives.

Seventy-three boats were wrecked off Redcar in the winter of 1820, and over thirty were wrecked or beached in one storm. One of the most tragic was the fate of the *Esk,* a whaler of 345 tons. Leaving the Tyne with only light winds, the captain hugged the shore to take advantage of the prevailing tidal currents. Returning from the waters off Greenland, Captain Dunbar was anxious to make his home port of Whitby. An on-shore gale sprang up on 7th September, 1826 and drove the whaler across the rocks to the east of Redcar. The boat ran ashore and quickly broke up. From the shore, watchers saw five or six men grasping at each piece of floating wreckage. Only three survived from the crew of twenty-nine.

THE PORT WILLIAM HARBOUR SCHEME

THERE was public concern at the lack of a safe anchorage along this hazardous coast. In 1833, Mr. William Richmond put forward the case for building a refuge harbour at Redcar. A public subscription was then started in the town to further this aim.

The scheme was the work of Mr. W. A. Brookes, a civil engineer from Stockton on Tees. After surveying the coast he found that the very rocks which had hitherto been such a hazard for shipping might form the natural base for a harbour. According to his scheme, the two parallel ridges of rock, Eastscar and Saltscar, would be extended a little further out to sea. Piers of solid stone could then be built along them, forming a sheltered harbour of 530 acres. The piers would project about one and a quarter miles out to sea; the entrance would be a thousand yards wide and thirty feet deep at low water. It would accommodate a fleet of Line of Battle ships or over two hundred coastal vessels. The obvious advantage of the scheme was that nature had done all the preparatory work in providing the foundations. Brookes estimated that the northern defence wall would cost £160,000 and the whole work £300,000. He also envisaged the provision of a third wall to the east of the Eastscar rocks thus making a second basin which would be reserved for naval vessels. The harbour was to be named "Port William" in honour of the reigning monarch.

The Bill for Port William was introduced to Parliament in 1839. It immediately met strong opposition from the Stockton M.P.s who feared, perhaps rightly, that Stockton would lose trade to Redcar. One of the most contentious clauses in the Bill was that causing a tonnage rate to be levied on all loaded vessels passing the port. The argument was that in times of storm, any passing vessel would be grateful for the port's existence, and the levy would also help defray the building costs. This clause was the undoing of the Bill and it was subsequently lost.

Twenty years later there was a further attempt to implement the Port William scheme. This time it was intended that the Port be linked with Middlesbrough by a ship canal to be cut through the Coatham Marshes. This would do away with the dangerous passage through the shoals of the wide Tees estuary and shorten the distance to Middlesbrough where the infant iron industry was growing at a prodigious pace. Again the scheme came to nothing. In 1859 came the report of the Harbour of Refuge Commissioners. They recommended the construction of three harbours; one at the entrance of the Tyne, one at Filey, and the other at Hartlepool. In preferring Hartlepool, the report stated:

> "Redcar, a place without trade or great commercial interests can contribute nothing to the expense of a harbour, whereas from Hartlepool, a flourishing port of daily increasing import-ance, extent and wealth, large assistance is to be expected in return for the advantages it will derive from its creation."

THE WRECK OF THE " CAROLINE "

CHRISTMAS day, 1836, brought sorrow to the people of Redcar. On that day the Zetland liftboat lost one of its crew. During a heavy north-east gale, the Danish brig *Caroline* was seen running for the beach at Redcar. Caught by the breakers beyond the Salt-scar rocks, her crew of nine took to their boats. They were all swept away before the lifeboat could reach them. The crew of the Zetland battled on, rowing through mountainous seas, seeking sur-vivors. As he was preparing to rescue one of the Danish sailors, William Guy was caught by a wave and swept overboard. He was the first and last lifeboat-man to be lost from the Zetland. All the Danish crew perished.

CHAPTER THREE — THE 1840's

BETWEEN 1820 and 1840 there were few changes in the two communities of Redcar and Coatham. Redcar continued to grow steadily; Coatham remained virtually static.

TOTAL POPULATION FIGURES

	Redcar	Coatham
1821	673	686
1831	729	663
1841	794	714

N.B. The Coatham Census figures include the whole of the Parish of Kirkleatham, but they reflect accurately the changes in the resort.

Redcar was still a quiet, select watering place. Its chief attraction was the beach with the broad expanse of firm, smooth sand. There were paddle steamer trips to Newcastle, Tynemouth, Sunderland, Hartlepool, Whitby and Scarborough. Country drives round the district lead the visitor to Wilton, Upleatham, Kirkleatham, Skelton, Guisborough and Ormesby. The following report of the summer season at Redcar is taken from the *Cleveland Repertory and Stokesley Advertiser* of August, 1843:

> "We were glad to observe that the fashionable watering place continues crowded with highly respectable families . . . All the lodging houses, and especially those of superior description, have been pretty full during the season, and the principal inns have had far above average patronage, although Mrs. Sowray's has stood first on the list." Mrs. Sowray kept the Red Lion Inn.

White's Directory of 1840 lists eighteen lodging houses at Redcar and there would be many more people who took in occasional paying guests.

There were no lodgings listed for Coatham in that year; the public hotel, where Hutton had stayed thirty years earlier, had become a farmhouse. Writing in 1841, Walbran states in his *Visitor's Guide to Redcar*:

> "Now, visitors no longer come to Coatham. The village seems much neglected. Only a few individuals who cannot find accommodation in Redcar, or who prefer privacy and seclusion are to be found there during the bathing season. The bathing

machines, so much in use there, have vanished and seem to have joined their rivals at Redcar".

FISHING

IN the second edition of 1848, Walbran gives a detailed account of the fishing industry at Redcar. The fishing grounds were reckoned to extend about twenty miles out to sea but in winter the fishermen rarely ventured more than five miles from the shore. There were about thirty-six cobles at Redcar and they were manned by about one hundred men and boys. The larger cobles were crewed by five men and were forty-six feet long; the cost of the boats varied between £30 and £40. The ordinary cobles were twenty-six feet long and generally rowed by three men. They were built at Hartlepool for between twelve and fifteen guineas. In the past three men would share the cost of the boat, but, according to Walbran, most of the fishermen owned their own boats by the 1840's.

Fish were usually sold on the beach as the boats came in. The primitive dialect and the cunning manner in which the bargains were conducted often afforded some amusement to visitors. The fish were chiefly sent to West Riding towns, after the arrival of the railways in that decade. Eventually Redcar fish found its way to Manchester, Birmingham, Nottingham and even to London. Besides the fishing cobles, there were fifteen or sixteen boats used by the pilots to guide vessels to Stockton, Middlesbrough and Hartlepool. Coatham, which had once rivalled Redcar had no cobles at this time; its fishing industry having merged with that of Redcar.

A small salmon fishery flourished in Coatham Bay and the Tees estuary. It was founded by a family called Gaunt in 1830. Their tombstone in Kirkleatham churchyard (north of the church) records their activities. The fish were caught in long nets stretched out into the sea. A separate small industry was the trapping of wild ducks. They were caught in decoy nets on Coatham Marshes (now almost covered by the new steel complex at Redcar).

An officer and six men of the Preventive Service were stationed at Coatham. They had a small armoury at the west end of the village. Walbran had too high an opinion of the neighbourhood "to believe that it is ever required". The days of smuggling had long since passed. Only the oldest people in the village could recall days when smuggled gin was sold relatively openly at a penny a glass.

THE COMING OF THE RAILWAY

THE idea of extending the railway line from Middlesbrough to Redcar was first proposed at a public meeting in the Crown and Anchor. The advantages to the town would be immense. If Redcar was to retain its importance as a resort, the railway was a necessity. Without the railway, Redcar would almost certainly lose its holiday trade to Seaton, Hartlepool and other bathing places. There was even a slight suggestion that the town had already lost a little of its former prosperity. The railway would do much to make the town more accessible; visitors from the south and west of Yorkshire would reach Redcar in under five hours travelling time, it was claimed. Rail transport would be a quicker means of carrying the fish to the great industrial towns of the West Riding where there was already a considerable market for Redcar's produce. A further argument put forward by the proposers was the same as used by the canal builders a century earlier—cheap fuel. Coal cost ten shillings (50p) per ton in Middlesbrough but it cost a further seven shillings and sixpence (37½p) to transport it to Redcar. The cost of transport by rail would be only two shillings per ton. As well as visitors in the bathing season, the railway would furnish cheap transport for all the general and commercial needs of the town.

An Act for extending the line was passed by Parliament in 1845. Work commenced promptly and the line was completed in eight months. The line had only two intermediate stations, between Middlesbrough and Redcar, at Cleveland Port and Lazenby Station (Warrenby Halt). From Middlesbrough the line stayed within sight of the Tees and passed north of Coatham Marshes, the sandbanks offering better foundations. From Marsh House Farm, at Warrenby, the line headed due east to an impressive terminal station in Redcar. The course of the line can still be easily traced along a deep gully running the length of the Cleveland Golf Course, thence along Queen Street. The station was situated precisely where Craigton House now stands at the junction of Queen Street and West Terrace.

The opening was a grand occasion. On June 8th, 1846, the procession left Darlington. Leading the cavalcade was George Stephenson's "Locomotion" which pulled fourteen trucks of coal and lime. Immediately behind was engine "A" of the Great North Eastern Company, pulling a passenger train of twenty carriages. Both engines carried the Union Jack. At Middlesbrough docks all the ships were decked out with flags. Large crowds were gathered all along the route, cheering and waving banners. The momentous journey took two hours.

As Redcar was developing, the neighbouring resort of Saltburn was being discovered. The directors and owners of the iron mines and iron and steel making companies sought pleasant resorts close to their industrial centres, both Redcar and Saltburn fulfilled those needs, as to a lesser extent did Marske-by-the-Sea. Within 15 years, the railway line was extended to Saltburn. West of Coatham, the line was diverted southwards and ran round the south side of Redcar. A new station opened with the line in 1861 and the old was left at the end of a spur. It stood empty for some while and was sold in 1873 as the Central Hall. A market was held inside. Alexander Coverdale leased much of the frontage facing the High Street and Queen Street. A man of divers interests, Coverdale ran a drapers, a gift shop, a jewellers and watchmakers, a circulating library and a printers and stationers.

Towards the end of the century, part of the old station was made into a theatre and in August 1893 or 1894 the D'Oyly Carte Company performed *The Mikado,* on stage. Later the hall was turned into two cinemas, the Central and the Regent. The former was destroyed by fire in 1948 and re-opened in 1954. Pantomime and variety shows were occasionally still performed at the Regent Cinema until that time. The building was demolished in 1964, and the Craigton House development superseded it.

THE WRECK OF THE " SUSANNAH "

IN 1841, the collier brig *Susannah* of Stockton was wrecked off the shore at Coatham. A large crowd was assembled to watch the rescue attempts. Before the lifeboat *Zetland* could reach them, the crew of nine were lost. Eleven other vessels came ashore near the same place in that storm, two were broken up, the remainder refloated.

CHAPTER FOUR — THE 1840's

THE railway extension to Saltburn had not been started so the line shown on the map is the original route from Middlesbrough, via Queen Street to Central Hall. About a mile outside Coatham was Upleatham Junction. A narrow gauge track ran up to the ironstone mines at Upleatham. It crossed Kirkleatham Lane, then Coatham Lane, under Red Bridge—Coatham Bridge; turning south, the track ran alongside Ramshaw's Lane or Low Farm Lane, now Mersey Road. Turning east the line came to West Dike Lane where it swung sharply south again. Turning east again, the route passed a stationary engine, presumably there to assist the passage of loaded trucks up the incline after passing under Redcar Lane. Thence the line turned south east towards the hills. The line to Saltburn was to follow much the same path and in places to use the same foundations. The low state to which Coatham's popularity as a resort had sunk can be gauged by the routing of the original line between the village and the sea and the extent to which the sidings spread over East Coatham.

Had it not been for the railway, Redcar would still have been a rather isolated place. The town could still be reached only from the south, via Redcar Lane. West Dike Lane was but a track. To the east there was a bridle path along the sandbanks and cliff-tops to Marske. Back Lane ran along the rear of the properties on the south side of Redcar High Street; crossing Redcar Lane it continued towards Coatham, running parallel to and south of Coatham High Street. This is now one of the main through routes across Redcar from west to east—Coatham Road, Milbank Terrace and Lord Street. In 1853 it ended at Coatham Lane, there being nothing but sandbanks and a rabbit warren beyond it. Warrenby was not built until twenty years later.

Coatham was reached along Kirkleatham Lane, then Coatham Lane, from the south. West Coatham Lane ran south of the marshes to outlying farms. This is now Broadway, Dormanstown.

Coatham marshes have seen much history. The Romans camped there, maintaining their chain of signal beacons; signals from Huntcliff beacon could be received and transmitted north towards Hadrian's Wall. The marshes were worked through ancient times to produce salt, traces of these old salt workings can still be seen, although soon they will be lost for ever beneath the relentless spread of the Redcar Works of the British Steel Corporation. There

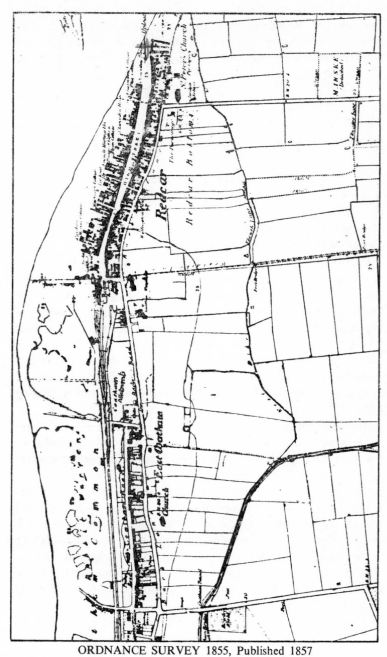

ORDNANCE SURVEY 1855, Published 1857

Part of 1: 10,560 Sheet, Yorks., N. Riding Sheet 7.
Reproduced from the Ordnance Survey sheet by permission.
Crown Copyright reserved.

37

was a regular trade in salt from Coatham to Guisborough Priory and thence to Whitby in the 12th to 15th centuries. In those days Kirkleatham was a flourishing community with several inns and much activity concerned with the passage of trade from the coast inland and along the main coastal road from Yarm towards Whitby.

The original Ordnance Sheet was surveyed in 1853 and published in 1857. The basic scale was six inches to the miles (1: 10560); there is insufficient detail to permit many particular buildings to be recognised. The census returns of 1851 offer more help.

CENSUS OF 1851

FULL names, exact ages, the relationship of each member of the household to its head, and the sex, occupation and birthplace of each person are all enumerated in the census. Thus an accurate picture of the community can be built up.

Half the people who lived in Redcar were born and bred there. A further thirty per cent came from towns and villages in the North Riding of Yorkshire. Of the remainder, most came from County Durham. More people came to Redcar from Guisborough than any other single place. This obviously arose from the age-old links between the two places. From earliest times fish from Redcar had been sold at Guisborough Market and salt from Coatham had started its journey inland along the same paths. Quite a number of people came from Stockton, another market town and a thriving port.

The census returns for Coatham present a similar picture. Forty per cent were born and bred Coathamians. The highest number of "off-comers" might have been made up partly of immigrant workers who had arrived with the railway and partly from visitors who had settled there when the village had been a popular spa forty years earlier. Most of the 'new' residents had come from towns and villages within twenty-five miles. Many were farmers and agricultural workers. It appears that there was more mobility of labour in the countryside than is generally supposed to have been the case. Of those not born in Yorkshire, most came from the fringes of County Durham—from Stockton, Darlington, Norton, Aycliffe and Bishop Auckland.

The occupations of most of the men of Redcar fell into one of three main groups. One fifth of the working men were fishermen and their sons. Almost as many were engaged in the building trade, a sure indication that the town was growing. The other main group comprised shopkeepers, merchants and craftsmen. Farmers and their labourers totalled twelve per cent and pilots, sailors and other seafarers made up a similar percentage of the male working population. Another small but significant group was that of those living from private income, usually land or house owners. The remaining group included male servants, grooms and coachmen. There were also a surgeon, two schoolmasters, a magistrate, a surveyor and several clergymen. Once built, the railway gave employment to only a small number of men.

Married women did not go out to work. Once married they became housewives, therefore the working female population was almost exclusively women without a man to support them. A large percentage of the widows and spinsters lived from private income; some were annuitants and fund-holders. Others owned property or land. In Redcar, many widows made a living as lodging house keepers. Most of the working women were employed in domestic service; they tended to be young, unmarried and "lived-in". Dressmakers, seamstresses and milliners formed the next most numerous group and a few women worked as laundresses.

Coatham was a very different picture. At the time of the census it was predominantly a farming community; well over one-third of the men worked on the land. The only other sizeable group was that of the shopkeepers and craftsmen. Surprisingly there are no fishermen recorded at Coatham other than the eight salmon fishers. Few women worked at all. Of those who did, most were dressmakers, and they were only thirteen in number. A small number of unmarried girls had come to Coatham to work as domestic servants mainly in the farmhouses.

Primary education was not compulsory at the time, nor was it free. Therefore, nationally, the majority of children did not attend school. The reverse was the case at Redcar where eight out of ten children attended school between the ages of five and twelve years. There were also a few described in the census as "scholars at home" —they had governesses. In only two families in Redcar, both those of fishermen, did the children not receive any formal education. At Coatham, education was free at the village school and all the children who were eligible attended. Consequently there was no recorded child employment, either on farms or in service. At Redcar, three children below the age of twelve were employed; two, aged nine and ten, were errand boys, the other, aged eleven, was in domestic service.

REDCAR

IN the middle of the 19th century, Redcar had become a small
town which was beginning to spill over beyond its one main
street. Houses had been built behind both sides of the High Street
in a rather haphazard fashion. Known as North Side and Back
Lane, they grew to become Esplanade and Lord Street. High
Street had been steadily growing but had not yet reached its present
length; the houses were numbered up one side of the street and
down the other. Building was under way at the east end of the
High Street as Albion and Clarendon Terraces came into being.
At the opposite end was a new hotel; the Railway Hotel had been
built diagonally opposite the old station, next to it were two houses
known as Railway Terrace. The hotel changed its name to the
Clarendon when the old station was closed. Zetland Square, popularly known then, as now, as Fishermen's Square, stood at the
eastern extreme of the town. The cause of the nickname was obvious, many fishermen lived there.

The houses in North Side were numbered 1-23 and there were
a further half-dozen or so cottages built amongst them. Three
side streets were developing between North Side and High Street.
Station Street was so named because the old station stood at its
corner, later it was renamed West Terrace; it comprised "The
Mason's Arms" and one house and the old Zetland School. Bath
Street took its name from the bathing establishment of James
Carter, situated along the west side of the street and nearest the
High Street; there were five other houses in that street. Moore
Street, then called Swan Lane had three houses.

Lord Street kept its old title of Back Lane until quite recent
times. Eleven houses belonged to the Parish of Upleatham; this
was the result of some ancient rights probably concerned with
fishing, owned by Upleatham. At least one prospective groom was
caught unawares by this anomaly; taking up residence in order to
be able to marry a non-resident lady, the young man discovered
to his chagrin that he had qualified to be married at Upleatham, not
Redcar Church. This detached portion of Upleatham was bounded
by the sea to the north, Lord Street to the south, Redcar Lane to
the west and stretched east nearly to Zetland Park. West of Redcar
Lane, there were ten cottages of which only one had a name; the
remainder were addressed simply as "The Cottages, Back Lane".
Some of these cottages appear to have been built in the large back-
yards of High Street houses. This would also have been true of

some of the cottages along North Side. Four houses stood in Wellington Place, about halfway along Back Street. Seven terraced houses had been built at the West Dike Lane end of Back Lane; they were known as South Terrace and four still stand. Altogether there were over thirty dwellings in Back Lane.

Church Street was at the bottom of Redcar Lane; there were twelve houses and a little distance away was the Parsonage. There was also the mill house and Redcar's six-sailed windmill.

COATHAM

THE village had changed little since Hutton's visit. It still had one long street, built only along the south side. The census of 1851 listed seventy-five houses along Coatham High Street, Marsh House (farm) and four houses nearby, making a total of eighty. The same figure as Hutton had estimated in 1810. Development was in its infancy in the mid-nineteenth century. The first new houses were in Victoria Terrace, now part of Coatham Road.

Many of these old names are still to be found around the town. They are preserved on plaques, some quite ornate, high on the fronts of the terraces. Look for them near the centre or at the ends just below the eaves. In Station Road you can find Newcomen Street; Queen Street has King James Terrace; Dundas Place was recently obscured by the new fascia of W. H. Smith's shop in the High Street; Hobson's Terrace is on West Dyke Road. There are many more to be found.

The old railway station was occupied by one family. Behind it, in splendid isolation on the sandbanks, roughly on the brow of the hill in Turner Street, stood Railway Terrace. It comprised four white brick houses for railway workers. They were later dismantled and rebuilt at Kirkleatham where they are now preserved by the National Trust.

At the corner of West Dike Lane and Milbank Terrace was The Green House, with a smaller house nearby. Coatham's windmill and mill house stood at what is now the junction of Station Road and Coatham Road. The United Reformed Church stands precisely on the site of the old windmill. Near the Lobster Inn were several more houses, one of which was the school house. At the corner of Rocket Terrace and High Street was another public house, the "Waterloo Tavern". There was considerable building in the long gardens behind some of the fishermen's cottages.

CHOLERA

REDCAR was no longer a small village. By the 1850's the need for sanitary reform could no longer be ignored. Cholera was the dread of Victorian England. It struck both rich and poor. In over half the cases the disease proved fatal. Death came suddenly, usually within twenty-four hours. Redcar belonged to the Guisborough Poor Law Union. The Medical Officer of Health was much concerned. He foresaw the dangers to health arising from the unsanitary conditions prevalent in the town. The problem was really one of persuasion and enforcement. There was no governing body for the town to pay for the improvements and enforce sanitation laws. He raised the matter of sanitation with the Guardians of the Poor. They ignored his recommendations.

In September, 1854, cholera broke out. There were twenty cases and eight deaths in the town. Seven of the deaths occurred in Fishermen's Square, which was described in the contemporary press as a very dirty and ill-ventilated place. The owner of the property was the Earl of Zetland.

The Earl of Zetland took immediate and drastic action. He ordered the whole of the square to be pulled down and replaced

with an entirely new street for the fishermen. It was a row of twenty-two terraced houses built "with every sanitary improvement calculated to prevent the recurrence of the disease". The row was directly to the south of the original square and called South Terrace. Today it bears the same name but it is still more popularly known as "Fishermen's Square". In the centre of the row is a lookout position from which a watch could be kept for fishing boats returning and in times of storm for vessels in distress. Behind the terrace is a row of bait-houses where nets and tackle would be stored and maintained. There are still several fishing families in residence.

The action of the Guardians was typically English. They formed a committee. This body met to inspect the nuisances at Redcar. A month later a Sanitary Committee was appointed. Its members were dutiful and known members of the community but it is difficult to determine what improvements they effected.

Typhus followed the cholera within weeks. The epidemic was confined to the poorer parts of the town. There were thirty cases in Back Lane with one fatality. There were two more deaths on North Side. The outbreak appears to have stemmed from Smith Street, a newly-built block at the east end of Back Street. In December, 1854, a petition was forwarded to the General Board of Health asking that the provisions of the Public Health Acts be applied to the town. The General Board sent Inspector Ranger to report on the conditions locally.

The report, made in 1855, shows how the insanitary state of the town led to the outbreak of disease. The Ranger Report makes fascinating reading. It shows Redcar as a rather smelly dirty place; not quite up to the idealistic pictures of the town drawn in the early guides and directories.

In the bathing season, water was obtained from a spring three and a half miles from the town. It was sold to visitors and the wealthier residents at the rate of a halfpenny a gallon. The majority of the residents were dependent on wells for their supply. These tended to be shallow—between four and sixteen feet—and often adjacent to cesspools. There were many instances of wells being infused with seepage from the cesspools. In one case the seepage was such that the water had to be filtered before use. For inhabitants without wells of their own, there was a public pump.

The town was without drains and sewers, except for those

43

leading to cesspools or ashpits. Those houses with water closets drained into the cesspools and the foul contents were allowed to escape and seep away as best as nature could provide. The cesspits behind the houses on North Side were in the sandbanks and only a few feet from the dwellings. On the south side of the town, the roadside gutters led the sewage to open ditches. It was then left to stagnate in the fields. A local builder stated at the time that the soil had become "putrid, foul and offensive and had been the great cause of sickness. Unless something is done to remedy the existing evils, the town will be ruined". Although water closets were found in the lodging houses, the usual convenience was the ash pit privy in an outhouse at the end of the backyard to each house. At one time in Fishermen's Square, one privy served ninety-five people. Hence the force with which cholera had struck. The last signs of the outdoor privies can be seen at the rear of Queen Street. Low in the walls are wooden frames, about two feet square, which formerly contained doors; now they are bricked up. The doors hinged at the bottom and the top swung outwards. Hanging on the inside of the door was a receptacle; with the door closed the bin would be positioned beneath the seat. Night soil was removed regularly.

When Ranger made his report, there was no scavenger, as the privy emptiers were called. The responsibility for emptying the ash pits lay with the occupiers of the property. A responsibility to which they did not take kindly, or attend to frequently. Refuse was thrown into the road, or the open gutters, or even simply left to accumulate. The Medical Officer of Health considered these accumulations a further source of disease.

During the previous decade, houses had been built quickly to accommodate the rapidly increasing population. The development was not fettered by building regulations and not checked by health authorities. Houses could and were erected with no regard for public health. Smith Street, source of the typhus, was a prime example, being a block of eight houses built back-to-back. Another block of back-to-back houses was Lynas Place, condemned in 1924 and still standing fifty years later. Small houses were being crowded into the yards and courts behind the High Street. Some of these can still be seen from the Esplanade and Lord Street. Then there was the original Fishermen's Square. The MOH attributed the cholera outbreak to "the very wretched principles on which the cottages had been built".

Inspector Ranger recommended that the Public Health Acts be applied to Redcar forthwith. This gave the ratepayers the right to elect a Local Board of Health which would be responsible for carrying out the necessary improvements in the town. The problems were not restricted to Redcar. A few miles away, the townships of Eston, South Bank and Normanby were enduring similar tribulations as they exploded into being with the arrival of the iron and steel industries. These Local Boards were the forerunners of the modern Councils.

REDCAR LOCAL BOARD OF HEALTH

IN June, 1855, a year after the typhus and cholera, the Redcar Local Board of Health was formed and modern Redcar began to take shape. The first problems to be tackled were, of course, those of drainage and sewerage. Next on the list was to be the provision of a good water supply—to be furnished from a reservoir to be built at Upleatham. The first of the Board's Minute Books covering 1855-60 is missing, the remainder are kept at the Cleveland County Archivist Office. The surveyor's letter book of that early period describes the situation.

The drainage of the town was completed within two years. The Board installed the main drains and each householder was required to pay for private drains to be connected to the system. One old lady who refused to comply with the regulations had the drains installed by the Board which then compelled her to pay for the work. Once the main drainage work was completed, it fell to the surveyor to investigate and deal with complaints of nuisance. There were several complaints about dung heaps in back yards and pig sties; one cesspool was described as "full of filth . . . and stunk awfully". Having endured a generation of squalid conditions, it required considerable effort to bring the poorer areas in line with the basic standards; there were reports of great quantities of slops and soap suds being thrown daily into the gutters of Back Lane, such that a special statute was called for, to restrict the practice.

The next improvement came in 1857 with the introduction of gas lighting. The first place to be illuminated was St. Peter's Parish Church. Then many of the business premises were lit up and a week later the street lights were lit. The gas was provided under a contract with the Redcar Gas Company. There seems to have been a certain status attached to having a gas lamp outside one's premises. There were many letters exchanged later in the century regarding the location of a lamp at the junction of West Dyke Road with Milbank Terrace and Lord Street; the church elders felt it would be of greatest use outside the Congregational Church; the landlord of the Royal Standard and the residents of the Green House all had similar views regarding their corner of the junction.

THE ZETLAND SCHOOL

THE present Zetland School was built at the expense of the second Earl of Zetland in 1859, and the scholars were transferred from the old school in West Terrace. The new building had a hall, a classroom and a house for the headmaster. It was attended by one hundred and thirty children. The school was examined annually by an inspector. In 1863 the inspector pronounced it to be the best in his district; the reports were forwarded to the Earl of Zetland. The close relations between the school and the church are indicated by the entries in the School Log Books which date from 1863.

"Examination this afternoon in scripture . . . the Vicar of Coatham conducted it in the presence of a great number of ladies and gentlemen of the neighbourhood."

Questions would include many things learned by rote, including the Ten Commandments, the Catechism, Creed and Lord's Prayer. Quite an ordeal for the children.

The headmaster's entries in the Log Books reflect the social changes occurring throughout the town. There are frequent references to the "season". School attendance would fall considerably during the summer as the older girls were kept at home to help with housework. Succintly, the headmaster wrote: "The girls are beginning to drop off, my 'summer' is passed and the town's is commencing." On another occasion he wrote: "Redcar is filling fast with visitors and the shopkeepers are getting every available boy to run errands. Several are driving donkeys and fully half of the girls are at home." In later years, Redcar Races proved to be another distracting magnet for the children; there were also the Regatta and Fair Days. With perhaps a touch of despair, the Log Book notes: "There was never such a place as Redcar for disturbing influences on attendance in summer-time".

Many entries refer to the shipwrecks which inevitably meant low attendance figures, either to watch the disaster as it occurred or to comb the beaches afterwards for jetsam. An entry in January, 1866 is typical: "Three ships ashore . . . half the school absent." The heavy deposits of sea-coal on the beach following a storm also diverted the energies of the children, as they helped their parents gather this free fuel. Sickness and disease still spread easily through the community despite the improved sanitary conditions. In 1870 the headmaster wrote: "Smallpox is proving very fatal among the children, four dying this week." Attendance was so low and the risk of infection so high throughout the town that the school was eventually closed for a month. The school was closed again in 1884 on the advice of the Medical Officer of Health, when scarlet fever raged through the town. The one direct reference to the Ironworks in the district comes in 1878, when the headmaster explains the fall in the number of pupils on the roll. Because of a depression in the iron trade, the population had contracted and many families had suffered very great distress during the previous hard winter.

School fees continued to be paid at the National Schools until late in the century. Free education commenced in 1891, but parents still paid sixpence (2½p) per quarter. Not until 1898 did education become entirely free.

In 1889, Her Majesty's Inspector of Schools reported that the accommodation at the school was insufficient for the size of the parish. Lord Zetland promptly came to the rescue and had the school considerably enlarged. Zetland School was maintained by the Zetlands until it was taken over by the North Riding County Council in 1904.

CHAPTER FIVE — THE 1860's

THE Plan of Redcar, 1861, was originally published as *Peat's Plan*, an advertisement for the chemist of that name, trading in the High Street, and appeared as a supplement to the *Redcar and Saltburn Gazette*. It was intended as a guide to visitors, with hotels and lodging houses marked along with several other places which would be of interest to the visitor. Mr. Peat's premises were in the High Street where Marks and Spencers now stands.

During the 1850's, a number of short terraces had been added to the existing streets. At the east end of the High Street, Albion and Clarendon Terraces had been completed and Granville Terrace laid out. At the west end, were North Terrace and Dundas Place. Marine Terrace, on the sea front, was to become part of the Esplanade. Portland Terrace in West Dike Lane and South Terrace in Lord Street had been built; by 1861 Back Lane had changed its name to that which we now know. Development was beginning to move out from the High Street; Albert Street was under construction and Alma Parade was being laid out. Most of the main streams of Christian beliefs had arrived. The plan shows that in addition to St. Peter's Parish Church, there were Congregational, Wesleyan and Primitive Methodist Chapels and a Friends' Meeting House.

Bathing was still an important activity. The nineteenth century fostered the creation of many special health resorts. Redcar competed with Harrogate and Bath by offering the 'medicinal' qualities of sea water. Dr. Horner's Hydropathic Establishment, near the Royal Hotel on the Esplanade was believed to be the only one in Great Britain using cold salt water to "cure all ills". Conventional hot or cold showers, or baths were available at the two other bath houses. The newsroom, with its daily newspapers, appears to have been roughly in the same place as Redcar's original thatched Post Office. For those who preferred indoor pastimes, the Red Lion, The Royal and the Zetland Rooms (later the Zetland Hotel) offered billiards.

A VISITOR'S HANDBOOK, 1863

TWEDDEL published his *Visitor's Handbook to Redcar, Coatham and Saltburn by the Sea* in 1863. Redcar had improved somewhat since Hutton visited the village in 1810. The mud-walled dwellings had given way to neatly built cottages (see those on the Esplanade between the lifeboat house and the pier ballroom) and handsome lodging houses. The appearance of the High Street had been improved by the removal of the low buildings in front of the old cottages; the mountains of drift sands had also been removed, making travelling less hazardous. "The spring cart of the farmer or tradesman and the chariot of the aristocrat now bowl along the street without the least impediment" notes Tweddel.

The improvements were such as to be rated as newsworthy by the *Middlesbrough News and Cleveland Advertiser.* On July, 27th, 1861 there was printed a report entitled *The Sea-Side—A Visit to Redcar.* The streets were no longer paved with sand; there were pavements in all the principal thoroughfares and leading down to the beach. The town was thoroughly drained and was dry and healthy. All this was the work of the Local Board of Health. The only fault the reporter noted was that the outlet of the main sewer was above the low water mark and that at times "unpleasant smells and noxious exhalations" wafted across the beach. Responsibility for cleaning the beach lay with the Local Board of Health. One Mark Baker successfully tendered in 1861 for removing all fish refuse from the sands.

The Local Board was concerned with improving the appearance of the town and particularly with increasing its attractions as a seaside resort. An early scheme was to have the old buildings removed from the middle of the High Street. The first major construction scheme was the building of a sea wall and promenade. Completed in 1869 it ran the full length of the existing town and permitted visitors, and residents, to walk out in all but the worst of weathers. The surveyor was instructed to procure twelve seats to be placed along what we know as the Esplanade; they were to be painted green. Redcar was developing and expanding at a brisk rate and it was apparent that some form of control was needed to enforce reasonable standards. In 1863 a committee was appointed to prepare Building By-Laws and to lay the same before the Local Board for approval.

Despite the improvements, some visitors were still critical. An unknown author, disenchanted with the town, penned the following in 1864 and addressed it to the "Good People of Redcar":

A PARTING WORD, or
REDCAR AS IT IS AND REDCAR AS IT SHOULD BE

"Redcar, the glorious sandy old town of one street, where the houses are as irregular, as unsystematic, as unarchitectural, as unconformable with each other as the most ingenious, botching house-planner could possibly contrive."

The sea front rated poorly too:

". . . with its zig-zag series of single-decker, higgledy-piggledy, gipsy-like hovels. The discharge pipes . . . whence everything that is disgusting and nauseous is constantly oozing under the very noses of every passer-by. Don't allow the shore to be made a continual muck-heap and you will have visitors in shoals."

The anonymous critic was correct in another of his assumptions: the roof line of the cottages on the sea front had been deliberately kept low so as not to impede the views for the High Street guest houses. Despite the efforts of the Local Board he found the town little improved, although he conceded that the supply of gas and water was progress. The benefits of the drainage and sewerage systems he found somewhat negated by the continuing habit of the natives to throw their domestic refuse "in filthy and disgusting rubbish heaps around the houses". After admonishing the residents sternly, he looked to the future.

His plan was quite clear. First, the residents should "pull down every one of those dirty, little one-storeyed excrescences"; in their place should be built a promenade of new terraces of lodging houses, overlooking the sea. The High Street should be reserved exclusively for shops. In addition, he felt that the town needed a market and a park where visitors could stroll would be a fine amenity. He hoped that his address would make the people of Redcar bestir themselves; he felt that they did not appreciate their own town, yet they had much of which to be proud. Although in some matters a full half-century ahead of his time, this critical visitor foresaw quite accurately the form in which the resort was to develop. The massive terraces were built along the front; the discharge pipes were extended much further out to sea; a market was established and survived several sites and variations in popularity until 1959; parks were established.

THREE FAMOUS VISITORS

NATHANIEL HAWTHORNE, an American whose works include *The Scarlet Letter* and *Tanglewood Tales*, stayed in Redcar with his family from July to October, 1859. They arrived by train from Scarborough and spent their first night at the Clarendon Hotel, it being adjacent to the existing railway terminus.

The following day they moved to a lodging house on the corner of King Street and High Street, where they boarded for the remainder of their stay. Hawthorne chose Redcar because he wanted a quiet location whilst working on the final draft of his novel *The Magic Fawn.* The town proved much busier than the family had anticipated. In a letter to her sister, Mrs. Hawthorne said: "We thought this would be out of the way and solitary but were much mistaken. It is, however, not quite so expensive as Whitby, which is more reasonable than Scarborough."

Charles Dickens was unimpressed by Redcar and described it as a "long cell". The story goes that he walked from the old railway station down to the beach. With carpet-bag in hand he cast one mournful glance at Coatham, another at Redcar, turned on his heel and walked back to the station. He was travelling towards Whitby and had elected to see the coast rather than use the established moorland route. Dickens made his way to Marske where he lodged overnight in the Dundas Arms (adjacent to the roundabout in Marske High Street where there is now a raised terrace of shops). His journey thence was not uncomplicated: the carrier who undertook to transport him to Whitby stayed so long to enjoy a parade with bands in Loftus that Dickens had to make an overnight stay in that town.

Samuel Plimsoll resided for a while in a house where Marks and Spencers now have a shop. Walking along the beach he could not fail to observe the "coffin ships". These old sailing vessels were all in poor condition and usually dangerously overloaded, their owners being anxious to carry as high a payload as possible. The boats attracted their nick-name from the frequency with which they foundered and the consequent high loss of lives. Plimsoll observed that the boats sank or rose predictably, as they were loaded or unloaded. As a result of his observations, a line was to be painted round the side of all vessels to indicate the loading capacity. The Plimsoll Line became law in the Merchant Shipping Act of 1876.

THE REVIVAL OF COATHAM

THE *Middlesbrough News and Cleveland Advertiser* reported in June, 1866 on the summer season at Redcar and at Coatham. The latter had not enjoyed a reported "season" for over three decades; that coincidentally was the time that the village was separated from the shore by the early railway line which had run to the old Central Station. By June, the season was well under way at Redcar and there were many visitors in the town. With more accommodation available at new lodging houses, a very busy summer was expected; three or four of the new guest houses were right on the sea front. The newspaper reporter describes the "magnificent houses, four storeys high, with uninterrupted views of the sea at Coatham", presumably Newcomen Terrace. Coatham Road then comprised a series of beautiful terraces and some villas, stretching from Victoria Terrace to Coatham Church, over half a mile away. There are more houses close to the new railway station; in all, accommodation for several hundred more visitors. The contemporary guides and directories again make copious references to the amenities of Coatham, no longer regarding it as a poor adjunct to Redcar.

The community had grown sufficiently to need and support its own church. Christ Church, Coatham was built in 1854 at the expense of Mrs. Newcomen of Kirkleatham Hall; most of the land in Coatham belonged to the Kirkleatham Estate. Mrs. Newcomen also provided the living for the priest and a further sum for repairs as they became necessary. Originally the church was under the care of the vicar of Kirkleatham, it was constituted a separate parish in 1860. Standing in splendid isolation, with the village to its north and Kirkleatham and the Cleveland Hills to the south, the new building soon became known as the "Church-in-the-fields". The beauty of the church impressed many. Tweddel declared it to be "decidedly the most beautiful church in Cleveland". St. Peter's church, Redcar was dismissed as "a poor affair" by the *Middlesbrough News and Advertiser*. The report continued: "Coatham Church is quite the reverse, being a handsome structure with an elegant tower and spire. A century of grime has dulled its beauty somewhat, or perhaps the twentieth century expects greater things: Sir Nicholaus Pevsner describes the same church as "dull . . . though remarkably, all the original stained glass remains intact".

Mrs. Newcomen was also patron of the Reading Room and Library which had a membership of sixty. The good lady also built and maintained a National School in 1866. Ten years later the management of the school came under the Kirkleatham School Board but reverted to the Church Authorities when the Boards were later abolished. Coatham Church of England School remained in use as a school until 1969 when it was replaced by a new building 100 yards away and the old building became a study centre for teachers. In the same year that Mrs. Newcomen founded the National School, the Society of Friends opened their Meeting House in Coatham.

Coatham's most famous school was Sir William Turner's Grammar School; one hundred boys, including twenty boarders were taught there. Sir William Turner was a wool trader of considerable standing in the City of London in the seventeenth century. He was President of the Boards of Bridewell and Bethlehem (Bedlam) Hospitals and was Lord Mayor of London in 1669. Having amassed a considerable fortune, Sir William founded in 1676 the almhouses known as Kirkleatham Hospital (rebuilt 1742). On his death in 1692 he bequeathed £3000 to create a free school. With the money, in 1708-9 Cholmley Turner built what is now known as The Old Hall, Kirkleatham. This generous building housed the school; the master lived in and received £100 per year; and the usher £50. In later years, the school was converted to a private house and the education of the children continued in the Hospital, which sheltered ten boys and ten girls, in addition to the score of old men and women. The Charity Commissioners ordered that the school be re-established and what was to be known as Sir William Turner's School was built on Coatham Road in 1869, where Redcar Central Library is now placed. (This building was replaced a century later when Sir William Turner's Grammar School was opened on Corporation Road, now Saltscar School. The name is preserved in Sir William Turner's 6th Form College on Redcar Lane).

The school built in 1869 was large and impressive. The east end first floor contained a chapel with a rose window. Below this room was the scholars' entrance and cloakroom. The central portion of the ground floor contained the large dining room behind an attractive colonnade; next to it was the kitchen with a huge fireplace. Above the dining room was a large library. The west end of the building provided living quarters for the headmaster and his domestic staff. Classrooms were above the library.

COATHAM CONVALESCENT HOME

REVEREND John Postlethwaite, first vicar of Christ Church, Coatham, bought a parcel of land from Mrs. Newcomen in 1860. On it he built and furnished Coatham Convalescent Home. The Home was built on 22nd May, 1861. It was a red brick edifice with courses of decorative blue and white bricks and was situated near the junction of Queen Street and Newcomen Terrace. There were magnificent views across Coatham Bay towards Hartlepool. The steady flow of sailing vessels into the Tees and along the coast would help the inmates of the Home pass the time. When opened, the Home accommodated fifty patients who were tended by voluntary workers. Later the Home was extended and a chapel built. A further wing was added to cater for mothers with their children; the Home became known as the Coatham Convalescent Home and Children's Hospital.

The patients were 'poor and respectable persons' recovering from sickness and requiring a change of air and sea bathing, mainly miners from County Durham. Subscribers and donors recommended patients for admission. A donation of five guineas entitled the donor to make one recommendation in that year; ten guineas, two recommendations and so forth. Annual subscribers could send one patient for every two guineas. The usual term of residence was one month, although this could be extended if thought necessary. Medical attention, board and lodge, washing and baths, and everything essential to the health and comfort of the patients were provided free of charge. Although founded by an Anglican priest, patients of all religious denominations were admitted; the only condition being that they attended morning and evening prayers conducted by the Church of England Chaplain. All the nurses and attendants worked on a voluntary basis, receiving no payment at all. The nurses were known as Sisters of the Home of the Good Samaritan; however, they were not necessarily members of a recognised Holy Order.

The Convalescent Home served its original function until shortly before the Second World War. During that war, troops were billeted there. After the war, Redcar Borough Council bought the property and in 1951 the home was demolished. A decade later, the Coatham Bowl was built to house an American-style ten-pin bowling alley. It is now a leisure centre.

CHAPTER SIX — THE 1870's

BEFORE the census of 1871, the Registrar General had suggested that in streets with two sides the houses should be re-numbered, one side having odd numbers and the other the even numbers. In December, 1870, the whole of the Redcar Local Board of Health met as a special committee to consider the re-numbering of property and the naming of streets within its jurisdiction. One small problem concerned that part of the town which still was under the control of Upleatham Parish; that part of the High Street kept its old numbers and the Upleatham portion of the Esplanade and Lord Street remained un-numbered. The High Street had more or less reached its present length by 1871. There were four new hotels, the Queen, the Globe, the Zetland and the Prince of Wales; none of which remain today.

Along the Esplanade there were more than twice as many houses as there had been recorded in the 1851 census. Some re-numbering had taken place and there were a number of cottages still known only by their name. There were seven houses in Lynas Place and six in Pybus Place. These thirteen houses were undoubtedly the darkest blemish on Redcar's sunny countenance; built back-to-back, they were crammed in to a space off the Esplanade, access was along a dark passage one metre wide. Even the Local Board's earliest building Bye-Laws prohibited such conditions; the houses had been built immediately prior to the enactment of the Bye-laws. The side-streets joining the High Street to the Esplanade were all in existence by 1871. Dundas Street ran where previously Pounder's Baths had stood. Three other new streets had been named; King Street, Graffenburg Street and Clarendon Street.

Lord Street appears to have been still developed on the north side only, apart from one or two terraces at its west end, as it had not been re-numbered. Many dwellings had been built in the large yards behind the premises on the south side of the High Street. There were six such yards, each with several houses or cottages. Unlike similar courts in other towns, the yards were not over-crowded, but the houses were very small and meanly constructed. Guy's Yard was the largest, with five houses. Many of these buildings still stand, now used mainly as store rooms or outhouses by the adjacent High Street properties; Two of these rough and ready buildings can be seen in Potts Yard at the rear of 118 High Street. (Remember that such places are private property and there is no public right of access).

Since the railway line had been extended to Saltburn and moved south, the land between the new line and Lord Street had started to be filled in with small squares and terraces. After Albert Street and Alma Parade on *Peat's Plan of Redcar,* came ten cottages in Wilton Street and two in Cleveland Street. Three houses known as West End filled the gap between the Clarendon and the Royal Standard Hotels; the beginning of West Dyke Road as we know it. Beyond the railway line lay only the gas works and gas house.

The growth of Redcar during the two decades prior to 1871 seems insignificant when compared with the explosion of development at Coatham. The small agricultural village had become virtually a new town. Unlike Redcar, the growth did not evolve from the old main street; new streets and terraces had been laid out, to a recognisable plan, across the common land which had separated the two communities.

The main development had taken place along what is now Coatham Road. It was made up of several individually named terraces, Milbank, Victoria, Cleveland, Portland, Marine, Bentinck and Vansittart. Amongst these new rows there were a number of villas and large cottages including the following: Clyde, Stanley and Wiltshire cottages and Grant, Clifford and Poona villas. On the south side of Coatham Road between the Grammar School and the cricket field stood Coatham Villas. These were the largest houses in Coatham, with long walled gardens to their south and with vegetable gardens beyond. Those that remain are now all public buildings. Those demolished have been replaced by a public library, a health centre, and a hotel. The largest of all the Coatham Villas is now an office of Langbaurgh Borough Council; earlier in its life it housed Redcar Borough Council. When these magnificently appointed homes were built they were for the wealthiest members of the community: Redcar was a popular dormitory for the families of the iron magnates of Middlesbrough and the south bank of the Tees.

The two terraces overlooking the cricket field merit special mention. This style of architecture was quite new to the district. Both terraces are almost perfectly symmetrical; Nelson Terrace has at each end a hexagonal turret with a spire. Opposite, Trafalgar Terrace is cement rendered and painted, instead of being white and decorated bricks, and has a dominating dormer gable in its centre.

Esplanade and Newcomen Terrace, 1890   Plate 5

Nov.ʳ 1812.

Subscribers to the Hearse, Built for the
use of the Townships of Redcar; Marsh and
Upsleatham. — This is a copy of the original,
Put up in Marsh Church on Sat.ᵈ the 9.ᵗʰ Day of Jan.ᵗ, 1813
~~~~~~~~~~~~~~~~~~~ by P Walton off.ʳ Statin'd at Redcar.

	£.	s.	d.
R.ᵗ Hon.ᵇˡᵉ Lord Dundas _ _ _ _ _ _ _ _ _ _	5	0	0
Hon.ᵇˡᵉ Laurence Dundas Esq.ʳ M.P. _ _ _ _ _ _	2	0	0
Jonathan Millner _ _ _ _ _ _ _ _ _ _ _ _	1	0	0
P Walton off.ʳ & Son _ _ _ _ _ _ _ _ _ _ _		1	1	0
Thomas Carleton _ _ _ _ _ _ _ _ _ _ _		10	0
John Trenholme _ _ _ _ _ _ _ _ _ _ _		2	6
Rob.ᵗ Simpson _ _ _ _ _ _ _ _ _ _ _		2	6
Mark Walker _ _ _ _ _ _ _ _ _ _ _		1	0
Eliz.ᵗ Hudson _ _ _ _ _ _ _ _ _ _ _		1	0
Jo: Dove _ _ _ _ _ _ _ _ _ _ _		2	6
Ch.ʳ Dobson _ _ _ _ _ _ _ _ _ _ _		1	0
R.ᵈ Hudson _ _ _ _ _ _ _ _ _ _ _		1	0
Thomas Burnicle _ _ _ _ _ _ _ _ _ _ _		1	0
Miss Allanson _ _ _ _ _ _ _ _ _ _ _		1	1	0
Jo: Wilson _ _ _ _ _ _ _ _ _ _ _		1	0
Rob.ᵗ Darnton _ _ _ _ _ _ _ _ _ _ _		1	0
John Horter _ _ _ _ _ _ _ _ _ _ _		1	0
Slater Potts _ _ _ _ _ _ _ _ _ _ _		1	6

card.ᵈ over

Public Hearse Subscription List — Plate 6

Hearse Regulations and Fees

The First Hearse Hirings

Plate 7

Spence's Victoria Baths, Coatham, 1884   Plate

Undoubtedly the finest home in Coatham, at that time, was "Red Barns". Built for the ironmaster, Thomas Hugh Bell, it was here that Gertude Lowthian Bell spent her childhood. A plaque on the north wall records simply that she was a "scholar, administrator and peacemaker. A friend of Arabs". The first woman to graduate from Oxford with a first in modern history, Gertrude Bell moved into diplomatic circles and fell in love with her "beloved east". Wherever she travelled, her notebook and camera went too. Regions hitherto unreached by Europeans were visited, surveyed and explored. Turning to archaeology, she established the National Museum of Baghdad. English to the end, Gertrude Bell dressed in European fashions; yet to the Arabs she was a great sheikh. At her funeral were great numbers of Arabs; their tribute—"If this is a woman, what must the men be like".

For half a century now, 'Red Barns' has been the house where the boarders of Sir William Turner's school have lived. Many past headmasters and their families have lived there too.

The middle strata of houses is represented by Newcomen Street, now Station Road; the houses were small enough to make impressive homes, yet large enough to be used as small guest houses.

Alongside the ostentatious houses, the humbler dwellings were growing in number. Pierson's Buildings stood near the junction of Ridley Street and Kirkleatham Street; these were twelve cottages, probably for labourers or agricultural workers. Pierson Street stretched for some length, discreetly behind the smart terraces of Coatham Road. In 1871 it was essentially a row of miners' cottages. Coatham High Street was linked to Coatham Road by Lobster Terrace; apart from these five houses, the old High Street seems to have stood apart from its new neighbours. It appears to have changed little in a score of years; there are the same number of dwellings as in the census of 1851. These were the homes of the local craftsmen and agricultural labourers; all that remained of the old village community of Coatham.

THE CENSUS OF 1871

IN twenty years, the population of Redcar had doubled. That of Coatham had trebled.

TOTAL POPULATION FIGURES

	Redcar	Coatham
1851	1032	456
1871	1943	1553

A new group of workers appeared in the census figures for the first time. With the discovery of ironstone in the Cleveland Hills, miners from all over the country had headed for the district. Every village and town within easy reach of the hills above Eston and Marske had a dramatic influx of newcomers. Whole new towns were created: New Marske, Eston, Grangetown, South Bank, all stretched along the south bank of the Tees and served the mining and iron-making communities. Over half of the miners who settled in Redcar were born outside the county; most came from Norfolk, Lincolnshire and Gloucestershire. This was the era of agricultural depression and falling wages for farmworkers. Many left the land to find richer pickings in industry. Many more of the newcomers were shopkeepers and craftsmen and tradesmen. This group made up one-fifth of the male working population. As in the earlier census, the next largest group were building workers. Despite the dramatic growth in the town, the number of fishermen remained static and in 1871 they were ten per cent of the working population. With the extension of the railway, the number of people employed by the railway company had risen, gate-keepers, points-men, plate-layers and several porters lived in the town. New professions to the town included a photographer and a jet manufacturer. Redcar had become a town of shopkeepers and lodging house keepers. Those who worked with their hands tended to be employed beyond the town boundaries. Domestic service was still the main occupation for the women of the town. There were still more situations than ever for domestic servants to tend the needs of the middle class occupiers of the new terraced houses and villas.

The structure of Coatham was more complex. With its return to public favour in preference to Redcar, the large comfortable houses catered more for professional people and "white-collar" workers. The largest occupational group was again that of the builders. Next came the shopkeepers and tradesmen, although far less in number than their fellows at Redcar. There were a few ironstone miners, half as many as at Redcar. Fewer men worked the land and lived in Coatham. Farmers and their labourers totalled less than eight per cent of the working population; this was probably the most significant change in the structure of Coatham and together with the loss of the fishing community two decades earlier, indicated the path along which the village would grow.

The working class accounted for half of the working population. The remaining half would all fall into a category headed "professional". It was a diverse group of clerks, agents, merchants, and brokers. Coatham had become the residential area for the merchants and industrialists of Middlesbrough amongst whom were to be found several iron-masters, ship-builders, iron-refiners, a brick manufacturer and the owner of a colliery. Thus established, the importance of Coatham and its residents increased steadily for the remainder of the nineteenth century. Although smaller in terms of actual population, Coatham was obviously more prosperous than the neighbouring resort; there were far more domestic servants employed and they tended to be specified as particular posts, such as nurses, cooks or housemaids. Very few Redcar households employed more than one servant, other than the lodging houses.

The arrival of the professional classes to Coatham no doubt raised the prestige of the place. This is reflected in its return to popularity as a resort. To the one lodging-house-keeper of 1851 had been added fifteen more by 1871 (in some instances one establishment was run by two sisters or two widows). Other widowed or unmarried ladies let off parts of their houses as furnished apartments.

THE IRON WORKS

UNTIL the 1870's, Redcar and Coatham had remained outside the area of industrial growth along the banks of the Tees. In 1873 an iron works was established about a mile from Coatham. There were six blast furnaces; the two blast furnaces of Coatham Ironworks, north of the railway line were erected by Messrs. Downey and Company: the four furnaces of the Redcar Works, south of the railway were completed the following year for Messrs. Walker, Maynard and Company. The opening of the ironworks was reported without great enthusiasm in the local newspapers. It was probably considered that the reputations of Redcar and Coatham as resorts would not be enhanced by publishing extensive details of the new industry and its proximity to the townships, in a district of previously unspoiled countryside. The press reports were short and insignificant.

"On Tuesday, No. 1 furnace at Coatham Ironworks was tapped for the first time, having been put in blast the previous morning. No. 2 furnace will be blown today."

Redcar and Saltburn News, 12th June, 1873.

It is difficult to ascertain the number employed at the ironworks in those early days; a newspaper report of 1895 states that there were around two hundred men at the Redcar Ironworks. The census of 1881 will show the breakdown of the trades and the origins of newcomers to the district. However, as this information remains secret for 100 years, the exact results of the census will not be made public until 1982. Some of the new iron-workers no doubt came from the building trades. By 1876, building was in recession at the two resorts as the initial explosion of development had petered out; many bricklayers, joiners and labourers could utilise their skills equally well in the ironworks. A number of Irish Roman Catholics had moved to the district seeking work, coincidental with the beginnings of the iron industry, the first Catholic school and church were built in Redcar. From living memory, there are recollections of skilled men coming from Staffordshire.

Blast furnacemen worked an average of eighty-four hours each week until almost the end of the nineteenth century. They worked a twelve-hour shift six days a week, with a twenty-four hour shift alternate Saturdays. The twenty-four hour shift, or "long turn", made possible the change over of shifts. Once each fortnight the men had Sunday off. There were no other holidays. In the early days, the work was not continuous and the pace was slow, otherwise the men could never have coped with the long hours or withstood the working conditions. Technical innovations in the 1880's speeded up the process considerably. Men throughout Cleveland demanded a three shift system. A decade later, 1897, most of the companies in Cleveland adopted the standard eight-hour shift.

The Cleveland iron industry was at its peak when Redcar and Coatham Ironworks were built. A depression followed, bringing hardship to the ironworkers and their families.

"Attention was called to the great amount of distress at present prevailing in the town (Redcar). The surveyor was empowered to obtain a supply of unbroken blue flint for road-making purposes and to employ any men who applied, to break the stone."

The Middlesbrough News and Cleveland Advertiser,

9th March, 1878.

A year later, the same paper carried the following:

"Attention has been drawn to the continued, serious distress among the poor of Redcar. Upwards of £50 has already been

dispensed by the church wardens in food, coals, and money:
and the Wesleyans have distributed soup and bread twice a
week."

Later in the century, in 1892, the strike by the Durham miners
brought more suffering to the whole of Cleveland. The strike lasted
three months and during that time every ironworker and miner
was thrown out of work through no fault of his own. By the third
week of the strike, the *Evening Gazette* reported that all the furnaces at Redcar had been damped down and the men were laid
off. They were luckier than many, as the owners, Walker, Maynard
and Company allowed the tenants of the firm's fifty houses at Warrenby, to live rent free for the duration of the strike. Downeys,
owners of the Coatham furnaces had been in financial trouble since
the depression and their two furnaces had been out of blast for some
years. Around the turn of the century, they sold out to Walker,
Maynard and Company. In 1915, Walker Maynard's was taken over
by Dorman Long and from then on the ironworks were known as
the Warrenby Works.

WARRENBY

BY September, 1873, a new village was emerging on the Kirkleatham Estate to house the ironworkers and their families.
"Where is Warrentown?" asks the *Redcar and Saltburn News* on
25th September, 1873. Then it continues, giving a favourable report
of the newly formed village. The cottages were erected by Messrs.
Robson, Maynard and Company on the main thoroughfare called
Tod Point Road. They were impressive and reported as being of
a standard above the common run of workmen's dwellings. Built in
terraces of seven, each cottage had a small garden under the front
window and a neat iron railing between the garden and the pave-
ment. Downey and Coney Streets were also mentioned in the newspaper report. The land was leased from Mr. A. H. Turner of Kirkleatham Hall. Warrenby virtually exploded into existence with
almost the entire village being built in a single wave of development. Building sites were everywhere. Some two hundred sites
had been leased, a site reserved for a school and a large hotel was
being built. To the south of Tod Point Road, the land was laid out
in small gardens so that each occupier might grow his own potatoes
and keep a pig. The village later changed its name to Warrenby as
it was thought that the 'by' suffix was more in keeping with the
many Danish influenced place names in Cleveland.

SACRED HEART CHURCH

BEFORE the 1870's, there were perhaps only around thirty members of the Roman Catholic Church living in Redcar. With the opening of the ironworks came many Irishmen and their families seeking work, bringing with them strong Catholic beliefs. In 1874, Canon Riddell held services at a small church in Lord Street. Three years later a new place of worship was opened for the Roman Catholic community. The first church of the Sacred Heart was built in Thrush Road and accommodated two hundred and twenty worshippers. Forty years later, the new Sacred Heart Church was opened in Lobster Road and the old building was passed on to the Methodist Church who still use it today.

CHAPTER SEVEN — THE 1880's

KIRKLEATHAM LOCAL BOARD OF HEALTH

AFTER the founding of the ironworks, the population of Coatham more than doubled, increasing from 1,615 in 1872 to 3,300 in 1876. Yet for all its rising importance, Coatham was still governed by Guisborough Rural Sanitary Authority. There was a growing feeling of dissatisfaction among the ratepayers of Coatham at this state of affairs. Having become a community of some stature and importance they felt that the governing powers should be placed in their own hands. A meeting of ratepayers was held in Coatham in 1876, to consider whether it was advisable to form a local board for the district of Kirkleatham. There was one notable absentee from the large, well-supported meeting; Mr. Newcomen of Kirkleatham was strongly in favour of the proposed local board, but did not wish to appear in the proceedings so that the ratepayers could feel free to arrive at a decision of their own accord. Financially, there was the question of whether or not they were willing to pay a rate of two pence in the pound and have the government in their own care. If they were not prepared to pay, then Guisborough Rural Sanitary Authority would remain in control.

As Redcar and Coatham had similar interests and common problems, it was proposed that a joint board be formed with Redcar. Due to the proximity of the two towns, indeed they merged together now, one surveyor, one clerk and one board room would suffice for both. The idea was rejected outright. Coatham was larger in population than its neighbour and it was common knowledge that the Redcar Local Board was in debt. A feeling of "them" and "us" was born and was to dominate many issues for the next half century. A poll was demanded. The results showed a large majority in favour of the formation of a local board for Coatham. A Local Government Inquiry was held in the National School in Coatham in July, 1876. The inspector was presented with the following resolutions which had been approved by a meeting of ratepayers:

"It is undesirable to separate or divide the parish in any way . . ."

"It is impolitic to attempt a union with the district of Redcar, especially as they have entirely different services of water supply and drainage. Also there is strong local feeling in the parish against such a union."

Then the evidence in favour of the proposed board was presented to the inspector. There were figures showing the increase in the population and the growth in the number of houses in the preceding four years. Mr. Newcomen added his support publicly. Recognising the difficulty of working efficiently from a distance, Guisborough Rural Sanitary Authority approved the proposition. There was a unanimous feeling among the ratepayers in favour of the new board. They sought greater powers to control the standards of building and the laying out of the streets and of the general sanitary arrangements of the town. They were also unanimous in wanting nothing to do with Redcar; Coatham was the select community, Redcar was a grubby, ill-planned resort.

"That difference was what the stranger failed to see," said the inspector. On entering Redcar he had seen a fence and been told that it was the boundary between the two towns. Without it he could see just one town, with but a common interest. The meeting could not agree with the inspector's observation. Coatham was residential, Redcar was a place of business; there were different classes of people either side of the fence. A novel reason for the separate boards, thought the inspector. He then clarified a misunderstanding; if united under a common board, Kirkleatham would not be involved in solving the debt of Redcar's existing board.

In November of the same year, Redcar Local Board of Health received the report of the Local Government Board Inspector. The report favoured the amalgamation of Redcar and Kirkleatham. The new board would have fifteen members, six from Redcar and nine from Coatham. Thus the new district of Coatham would take control of its established neighbour. Fearing amongst other points, a loss of control, a rise in rates and being unable to find any advantages in the proposal, the Redcar Board unanimously opposed it. No immediate decision was made. The local Government Board wanted to look further into the feelings of the people of Redcar and Coatham. The two towns agreed to differ. At a meeting of the ratepayers from both sides of the fence, a unanimous decision was reached—against amalgamation.

In July, 1877, the provisional order was received constituting the Parish of Kirkleatham into a Local Board district and an election was arranged for 1st September. There were thirty candidates from whom the following nine were selected :

Thomas D. Ridley, contractor; John Proud, farmer; James Rutherford, land agent; Edward Robson, mine owner; John Hikeley, inn-keeper; Thomas James, ironworks manager; Arthur H. T. Newcomen, Gentleman; Peter Wallis, farmer; Wm. Nelson, builder. Arthur Henry Turner Newcomen was unanimously elected Chairman.

The Kirkleatham Local Board of Health wasted little time in taking hold of the reins. It first met in the Lobster Inn in November, 1877. Subsequently meetings were held in the National school. The chairman of the Board was very much the father of Coatham as we know it. Due to his foresight, the sanitary arrangements were good, having been laid down to his plans in 1865. He had also exercised strict control, prior to the Board's creation, over buildings. Such was his influence that the streets between Queen Street and the sea were to be named Arthur, Henry, Turner and Newcomen streets. Water was supplied to most of the Kirkleatham Parish from the Stockton and Middlesbrough Water Company. The Inspector from the Local Government Board remarked that Coatham was more modern, better laid out and had better width of streets, more regular buildings and better footways, than its poor relation.

An early task for the Board was to arrange for the scavenging of the night soil from the privies. Tenders were invited for the work and the manure was to belong to the Board and to be sold by auction. The year was 1877. The following year the Board undertook to clean the streets and arrange with the Water Company for a supply of water for this purpose. In February, 1878, the sewers were improved by the addition of six ventilators. One still stands, a high cast-iron pipe, at the junction of Queen Street and Newcomen Terrace.

Relationships between the two neighbouring Boards appeared to improve little over the years. In 1879 they agreed to purchase a fire engine to serve both towns but the joint venture was, predictably, doomed to failure. Four years later, the Minute Book of the Kirkleatham Board records:

> "As the Redcar Local Board have refused to confirm the rules and Regulations of the joint Fire Brigade, the Fire Engine Committee is to be dissolved and immediate steps are to be taken to purchase and house a fire engine and organise a fire brigade at the expense of this district alone."

A fire station was built in Pierson Street. When a new fire station was built in Coatham Road in the 20th century, the old depôt housed the council's dust-carts.

REDCAR LOCAL BOARD OF HEALTH

IN the summer of 1870, smallpox broke out in Redcar and quickly spread throughout the town. A local doctor opined that the epidemic might have been prevented by prompt action from the Local Board of Health. Initially the Board took no action. When the first case came to the doctor's attention, he reported it to the Board asking for money to employ a nurse. He received no response. "Had it been otherwise I would have no hesitation in stating that it would have prevented what afterwards developed into a severe epidemic simply from the fact that the case had to be nursed by his relatives and willing friends who, not understanding my caution, surreptitiously gave their aid," wrote the frustrated doctor in the Evening Gazette. Finding themselves in the middle of an epidemic, the Local Board called a meeting of medical men, to ask advice; by then, though, the disease was prevalent in all parts of the town. Some good did come from the sorry episode. Realising the importance of prevention of disease, the Board appointed a Medical Officer of Health for Redcar. He was to advise on precautions that might be taken to forestall further outbreaks of disease.

The minute books record the reports of the annual inspections into the town's sanitary conditions. The report of 1872 states:

"After careful house to house visitation in which every ash pit, privy, sink and W.C. was examined, we have to report that the sanitary condition of Redcar is better than we have been accustomed to find it at similar annual inspections. The few exceptional cases are those of old property built before the existence of the Local Board. The yards are too small and so the privy and ash pit accommodation are inadequate."

The landlords were ordered to make the necessary improvements. The report went on to emphasise the need for a public scavenger and concluded :

"If these improvements are carried out, the sanitary condition of Redcar will be found in all respects satisfactory."

The inspector was in a delicate position; to criticise the conditions too severely was to imply neglect of purpose by the Board which employed him. The state of Redcar was still far from satisfactory and a further two decades were to pass before conditions generally became acceptable.

In 1876, Redcar applied for an extension of the district to include that part of the town which still came under the care of Upleatham; this was granted a year later in accordance with the petition of the Local Board of Health.

REDCAR RACECOURSE

HORSE races had been held on the sands at Redcar for many years. Local sportsmen competed for small prizes — a saddle, a bridle or a few sovereigns. A bathing machine served for the judge's box and a farm wagon for the stewards. Feeling that horse racing at Redcar had greater potential, an enterprising group formed the Race Committee in the middle of the 1800's. Its purpose was to introduce racing on more ambitions lines. Sufficient money was raised to offer stakes large enough to attract competitors from further afield, from Middleham, Richmond, Malton and Hambleton. The venture was a success. Redcar Races gained a new status and were included in the Racing Calendar. The races continued to be held on the sands until 1870 when they could no longer be held there for financial reasons.

The Race Committee leased land from the Newcomen family. The present racecourse was laid out in 1871 and the first meeting was held in 1872. Admission charges were two pence to the course and six shillings to the Grandstand enclosure. Three years later, the Redcar and Coatham Grandstand Company was formed. Their first decision was to build a new stand worthy of the meeting, this would replace the wooden stand which was dismantled after each meeting. During the same year, the course was improved. Arrangements were made with the Earl of Zetland for the extension of the course allowing for the inclusion of a straight mile in the course; this gave some added prestige to Racing at Redcar. Until the turn of the century, most prize money was about £100; total prize money in 1946 was £8,450 and in 1964 it had risen to £72,550, and in 1976 it topped £133,500.

The firm foundations and the early, and continuing success, of Redcar Races is attributed by the late Major J. Fairfax Blakeborough to the loyalty and enthusiasm of the local landowners— the Zetlands, the Newcomens and the Lowthers of Wilton. Since the Second World War, Redcar has led the world with innovations which have become accepted as the standards now; the publicly visible timing clock, the furlong posts, closed circuit television in colour are but a few.

THE PIERS

THE Redcar Pier Company was formed in 1866 with the intention of "providing Redcar with a commodious promenade and landing pier. The plans lay dormant until 1870 when a rival scheme for Coatham was proposed. A suggestion that a central pier be built to benefit both towns was never actively pursued; each group wanted the pier sited in their town. A compromise proved impossible, each resolved to build its own pier.

Redcar's scheme was financed by the selling of shares and, of course, the Earl of Zetland made a generous donation. The first pile was driven by Admiral Chaloner of Guisborough on 28th August, 1871, and the structure erected by Messrs. Head Wrightson of Stockton. The completed pier was 1,300 feet long and stemmed from the Esplanade, opposite Clarendon Street. The entrance was twenty feet wide and the gates were flanked by toll-collectors' offices and ladies' and gentlemen's rooms and a shop. The pier head was 114 feet wide and featured a bandstand with sheltered seating for seven hundred. There was a small landing stage at the pier head from which paddle steamers ran pleasure cruises

along the coast and plied regularly between Middlesbrough, Redcar, Saltburn and Whitby, Bridlington and Scarborough.

Shareholders had their hopes of regular dividends dashed by a succession of mishaps. At the end of October, 1880, the brig *Luna,* driven by storms, cut through the pier. Repairs cost the pier company £1,000. On New Year's Eve, 1885, the S.S. *Cochrane* demolished the landing stage and the pier company was unable to bear the cost of the repairs. Further damage occurred in January, 1897, when wreckage from the schooner *Amarant* swept against the pier stanchions. The most damaging blow came in the summer of 1898. Late on the night of August 20th fire broke out and the pier head was burnt down following a concert party. It was believed that the fire was caused by a wax vesta which had fallen, unextinguished between the planks. The bandstand was not rebuilt but was replaced by a mobile bandstand on the promenade. The total damage bill was between £1,000 and £1,500. In 1907 a pavillion housing a large ballroom was built near the entrance to the pier. It was extended landwards in 1928 and the minaret kiosks were absorbed into the frontage of the ballroom.

A deliberate breach was made in the pier in 1940. This was to hinder the enemy in the event of invasion. During the War, a mine exploded near the pier considerably weakening the structure which was already much decayed through neglect. After that, succeeding storms washed away almost the entire structure. The stump of the once magnificent pier projected only some fifteen yards beyond the Pier Ballroom, and remains much as we see it today.

Coatham pier was intended to outstrip Redcar by some 700 feet. Originally planned to be 2,000 feet long, it had the dubious distinction of being wrecked before it was completed. Work commenced in 1873. In December, 1874, two vessels collided with it. The brig *Griffin* was running north before a storm with a cargo of oak; the lashing wind and rain reduced visibility and the crew failed to see the unfinished seaward end of the pier. As the vessel slewed through, the crew escaped by jumping on to the pier. Later in the same storm, the schooner *Corrymbus* was driven through the pier and was a total loss. The cost of repairing the work was such that it was deemed wiser to shorten the pier by 200 feet to reduce the overall cost. The work was completed and the pier opened in 1875. It had two pavilions, one in the middle for band concerts and one near the entrance which housed a roller skating rink.

The pier joined the sea front opposite Station Road, then Newcomen Street. It continued to be dogged by misfortune and its demise came in October, 1898, when it was almost completely wrecked by the barque *Birger*. The Coatham Pier Company, already in financial difficulties through the cost of earlier repairs, could not afford further repairs on the large scale necessary to restore the pier. Instead they dismantled the severed, seaward portion. The following year the Pier Company ceased trading and the pier was allowed to disintegrate.

At the beginning of the present century, the then local authority erected a glass shelter over the old skating rink and gave the place a new lease of life as "Cosy Corner", the home for some years of Billy Scarrow's pierrots. In 1928 the "glasshouse" as it was known (a description still heard occasionally in 1976) was rebuilt as a theatre and called the New Pavilion. When the old Central Hall with its cinemas was demolished on 23rd July, 1964, the "New Pav" was converted into the Regent Cinema.

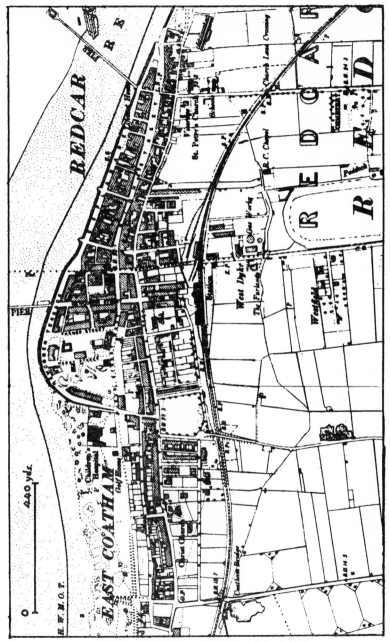

ORDNANCE SURVEY 1893, Published 1895

Part of 1: 10,560 Sheet Yorks., N. Riding VII N.E.
Reproduced from the Ordnance Survey sheet by permission.
Crown Copyright reserved.

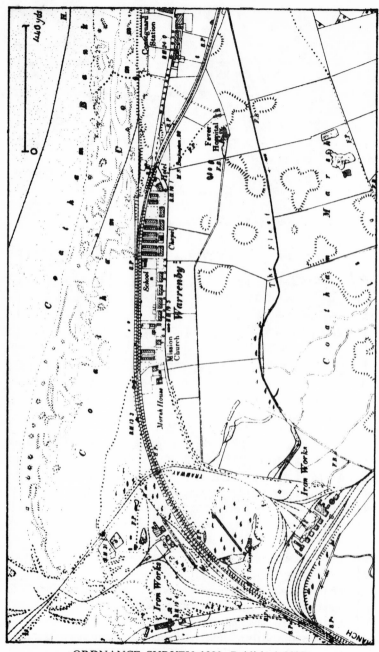

ORDNANCE SURVEY 1893, Published 1895

Part of 1: 10,560 Sheet Yorks.. N. Riding VII N.W.
Reproduced from the Ordnance Survey sheet by permission.
Crown Copyright reserved.

72

CHAPTER EIGHT — 1881 - 1900

THE second Ordnance Survey Map of the district was published in 1895 and it presents the last officially published picture of the area in the 19th century. By then, Coatham had been more or less built up as far as the railway line. Several terraces had been built south of Coatham Road. Overlooking the cricket ground was Trafalgar Terrace and behind that, St. Vincent's Terrace. Along Kirkleatham Street were several villas which now form the Stead Memorial Hospital. Another new street was Westbourne Grove and construction was under way in Henry Street and Turner Street. Few new working class dwellings were built in Coatham, there were only two short terraces of ironworkers cottages—Grant Street and North Terrace.

The building of working class homes was more widespread in Redcar. Almost all the new cottages were built in the four years 1872-76; this was the time during which the ironworks was being established. During this time, existing rows were completed in Alma Parade, Albert and Wilton Streets and Cleveland Terrace (the latter is now Railway Terrace). A number of new streets were planned in 1873-74. North of the railway line work started on Red Lion and Regent Streets and Regent and Fairbridge Places. South of the railway there were Birdsall Row and Herschell and Elton Streets. There was also new building work in Portland Terrace in West Dyke Road.

The building boom was over by the spring of 1876. Then followed a recession in the building trades until 1893. During those years Redcar changed very little. The new streets were laid out but not completely developed; Elton Street had only four houses and Birdsall Row had none according to the Ordnance map. The decline in the iron trade in the 1880's and the miners' strike of 1892 had brought the town's growth to an abrupt halt. What development there was, was closely controlled by the Local Board which insisted on its conditions being met and the bye-laws observed. The plans for Red Lion Street had been rejected five times, amongst the reasons given, it was pointed out that the proposed roadway was only twenty-four feet wide and the bye-laws required thirty feet. The sixth plan was approved in May, 1873, the year following the original application for planning approval.

JOHN SPEAR'S REPORT

IN 1885 a *Special Report on the Sanitary Condition of Redcar —with reference to its state of preparedness to withstand the invasion of cholera* was prepared by John Spears. The report deals initially with the defects in the sanitary arrangements. There was criticism of the haphazard way in which the sewers had been laid out and of their poor ventilation. Due to the flatness of the land, there was very little fall on the sewers. To keep the channels free, catch pits had been inserted and were emptied only once or twice each month. These pits were malodorous and ill-maintained. Some branch sewers were rendered even less efficient by acumulations of deposits. Private drainage needed considerable alteration. It was recommended that drain pipes be removed from within or beneath dwellings. Water closets were still found only in the better properties and the larger lodging houses. In the poorer parts of the town privy middens were still in general use, often in a "very dilapidated and foul condition." There were a few pail closets which were a slight improvement on the middens. Some arrangements had been made for refuse disposal but scavenging of the privies was not dealt with systematically; often calls were only made after complaints.

The water supply was, on the whole good, although sometimes insufficient. Much water was lost through the leaky and worn out mains. There were still a few local wells but these supplies were of doubtful quality.

The poorer dwellings were in a most unsatisfactory state. Many were very damp, some were so delapidated as to be classed as unfit for human habitation. There were several very small cottages which were overcrowded. Many of the newer houses and cottages for the artisans were found to be jerry-built. In the poorer parts of the town, the yards were described as filthy and dilapidated. There were several undedicated streets which had not been adopted by the Local Board. Common lodging houses were not registered in any way and were regulated by the police. They were all found to be overcrowded, ill-ventilated and dirty.

Criticism was levelled at the Local Board of Redcar itself. Its work was inefficent, its bye-laws were outdated and inadequate. The Medical Officer of Health was old and feeble and underpaid. His reports were meagre and of no value. The work performed by the Inspector of Nuisances was "as fair as can be expected under the circumstances." There was neither a hospital nor ambulance in the town and no arrangements had been made in anticipation of cholera striking.

Later in the same year, John Spears turned his attention towards the conditions in Kirkleatham District. The report implies that generally Coatham was in a better state than Redcar. The homes of the poor were as a rule "fair"; there were many complaints of dampness in the older property. There were no cases of over-crowding in the poorer households and there were no common lodging houses in Coatham. The sewers were kept free of accumulated deposits by regular flushing but their ventilation needed improving. Spears criticised the layout of some parts of the town; some small blocks of dwellings were so arranged as to restrict the free circulation of air. In one or two instances yards had been built over.

Turning to the activities of the Sanitary Authority and its officers, Spears' report is word for word the same as his report on Redcar. As in Redcar, he found neither hospital, ambulance nor any plans for dealing with cholera.

Acting on Spears' report, in December, 1885, Redcar Local Board of Health entered in its minutes that it intended taking steps to borrow money to finance various public works. The money would be spent on, amongst other things, replacing the water main from the reservoir to the town and a scheme for supplying the town with salt water for cleaning the streets and flushing the sewers. In March, 1886, the Clerk was instructed to serve notice upon the owners of property in the following streets to level, pave, flag and channel them: Alma Parade, Red Lion, Regent, Wilton and Back Streets and Wilton Place. Most important of all, the Board began to take more vigorous action against the owners of insanitary property on the following lines :

" Notice to be served on —— ——, owner of cottages 40 and 51 Lord Street, because the property is damp and dilapidated."

" Notice to be served on —— ——, stating that his eight houses in Smith Street are in such a state as to be unfit for human habitation."

In the latter case, the owner was given twenty-one days to make improvements, in default of which, proceedings would be taken to prohibit the use of the premises for human habitation. The main improvement in Coatham's sanitary condition was in the arrangements concerning the privies. The Kirkleatham Local Board of Health recommended that the pan system should be adopted in all cases where nuisances were reported from privies or ashpits. As a result of this, notices were served on owners of property in Station Road, Pierson Street and Pierson's Buildings requiring them to provide ash pans. The Kirkleatham Board also took steps to provide a hospital. In 1888 a house known as the Weigh House was converted to be used as a Fever Hospital; the building stood in isolation, well back from the road between Coatham and Warrenby.

In September, 1892, came a special report from the Local Government Board concerning the threat of cholera. Attention was drawn to the fact that Redcar still had no accommodation for isolating cases of infectious disease. The Board was prepared to wait until it was absolutely necessary before spending money. Six years passed before isolation accommodation was provided for Redcar, then only when the Board was spurred into action by the threat of an epidemic. In 1898 smallpox was raging through Middlesbrough and the neighbouring towns. To no-one's surprise, the Medical Officer of Health of Redcar eventually received notification of a case of smallpox in his district.

The advisability of isolating the case was discussed and it was decided to act jointly with Saltburn and Marske Councils and provide a joint hospital for the people of all three towns. A site was suggested on Hob Hill at Saltburn, well isolated and with plenty of fresh air. Saltburn Board were not fired with enthusiasm at the proposition. As they saw it, there was already a case at Redcar, though none at Saltburn. If the case was isolated at Saltburn, it would be said, rightly enough, that there was smallpox in the town, which might damage its image. Moreover, if there were many cases from Redcar, the hospital may have to be enlarged and Saltburn would have to bear some of the cost, even though none of the cases came from their own district. Finally the Marske deputation suggested a site at the foot of the Upleatham Hills (near the junction of the A174 and Redcar Lane). This location was well isolated and readily accessible from Marske, Redcar and Saltburn. The site was approved and plans were passed immediately for a building of wood and corrugated iron to accommodate six patients. The building was erected within the week. The case was isolated and the epidemic averted.

ENTERIC FEVER IN COATHAM

IN 1893 Doctor Barry reported to the Local Government Board on *Enteric Fever in the Tees Valley Towns*. There had been two outbreaks, each lasting about six weeks; 7th September to 18th October, 1890, and, after a brief respite, from 28th December to 7th February, 1891. There had been hundreds of cases of enteric fever in Middlesbrough and Stockton, causing the death rates of those towns to rise alarmingly. Other districts affected included Darlington, Ormesby, Normanby and Eston, the rural districts of Stockton, and Kirkleatham district which included Coatham of course. Dr. Barry made a careful and detailed examination into the sanitary conditions of each of the affected districts.

In Kirkleatham, he noted first the character of the district. The inhabitants of Warrenby and Dunsdale were employed chiefly in the ironworks and ironstone mines; those of Kirkleatham village worked on the land; Coatham he described as a residential resort with much rented accommodation. These activities were reflected in the type and mixture of housing in each community. At Dunsdale and Warrenby most of the dwellings were classed as cottages; at Coatham, less than a quarter of the houses were for the working class. Dr. Barry found the town of Coatham to be well laid out, with most of the houses of a superior class. As a rule there was sufficient space around each house; however, he too noticed that in some parts of the town there were blocks of houses placed so closely as to restrict the movement of fresh air and that yards had been built over. He found the main roads in the district had been macadamised and apparently well kept. The back streets of Coatham were satisfactory but at Warrenby "they were unpaved, unmade, unswept and frequently filthy." Little fault was found with the sewers and Barry reports that they were flushed with salt water daily in summer and twice weekly in winter. Most of the houses in Coatham had flush toilets, the rest of the district had midden privies or pans.

Water for all the houses in Coatham and Warrenby came from the Tees through the works of the Stockton and Middlesbrough Water Board. The villages of Dunsdale, Kirkleatham and Yearby, and all the outlying farms were dependent on wells and streams for their supply. This was the crucial factor. All the incidents of disease in Kirkleatham district occurred in Coatham and Warrenby; not a single case was reported at the villages of Kirkleatham, Yearby and Dunsdale. In every district where the disease struck there was a single, obvious common factor, the Tees. It was noted that the outbreaks both followed heavy flooding of the river. The Tees acted as a common sewer for all the places along its banks. Dr. Barry commented :

> "At Barnard Castle almost everything had been contrived so as to ensure, to the fullest, the fouling of the river by every conceivable form of filth."

The scene was also visited by the Kirkleatham Board of Health and they reported in detail in their minute book of June, 1893 :

> "We found on the Durham side large accumulations of filth of every description, such as ash pits refuse and human excrement from privies and closets, also several drains discharging into the river."

The Yorkshire side was just as deplorable. They also found "a huge heap of rubbish looking for all the world like a giant ash pit." Their final comment :

> "From looking at the high water mark on the bank, it is certain that all the filth will be washed into the stream at the first flood and carried to the Stockton and Middlesbrough pumping station."

COATHAM'S WATER SUPPLY

FOR some years, the Kirkleatham Local Board had received complaints about the inadequate water supply in the district. Drains were not always effectively flushed and there were many complaints of bad smells. The water pressure was insufficient for water to reach water closets on the upper floors of the lodging houses, particularly worrying in warm weather when the houses were full of visitors. Coatham was at its peak as a resort and its reputation as a healthy place was important.

Correspondence with the Stockton and Middlesbrough Water Board proved ineffectual. The Kirkleatham Board decided to transfer its supply from Stockton and Middlesbrough to the Cleveland Water Board. They applied for the sanction of the Local Government Board to borrow money with which to purchase the pipes, mains and fittings within the district belonging to the Stockton and Middlesbrough Company. When the first application was refused, further attempts were made, much emphasis being laid on Dr. Barry's report and the effect of Tees water in causing the fever outbreaks. Eventually consent was obtained.

The Kirkleatham Local Board served a notice on the Stockton and Middlesbrough Water Board compelling them to sell all the mains, pipes and fittings within the district. There followed a legal struggle. The Water Board rejected the offer made by the Kirkleatham Board of £2,669. An arbitrator was appointed by the Local Government Board; after hearing both parties he fixed the price at £25,422. The arbitrator had based his award on the revenue which the Water Board would have received from Kirkleatham, not on the actual value of the equipment. Shocked, the Kirkleatham Board appealed to the High Court and their appeal was upheld. The Water Board then appealed against the findings of the High Court; on 31st July, 1893, their appeal was dismissed by the House of Lords. Arrangements were swiftly made and from August, 1893, the Kirkleatham District received its water from the reservoir at Lockwood Beck, through the works of the Cleveland Water Company.

THE WARRENBY BOILER EXPLOSION

A TERRIFIC explosion shook the district on the 14th June, 1895. At Redcar Ironworks, thirteen boilers had exploded killing four men outright and injuring many more, some fatally.

The explosion came at about supper time. The furnaces had been tapped and many of the men were in their cabins for the first meal of the night shift. One of the boilers overheated, causing a seam to rip, and then exploded. A chain reaction followed as boilers, weakened by the first blast, exploded hurling metal, bricks and masonry high in the air. Men were buried under the rubble. Others were caught in jets of steam or scalded with showers of boiling water.

In Warrenby they first heard a low rumbling, followed by a low thud. Eye witnesses saw a huge globular cloud rising from the works. There was much alarm and the whole village rushed to the works. Bodies were to be seen everywhere. Rescuers were surprised to find so few dead; but many of the injured were badly maimed. Doctors and nurses worked all night alongside the rescuers administering what aid they could to those who had been scalded and crushed. The injured were taken to the Cottage Hospital at North Ormesby.

The death toll mounted to eleven as the days passed, the local men were buried in Coatham churchyard. At the inquest it was said that the explosion was unparalleled in the country. The verdict was "death from injuries resulting from the bursting of a boiler which had become overheated." No negligence was found on the part of the company regarding the maintenance of the boilers.

THE WRECK OF THE "AMARANT"

R EDCAR has its own *Marie Celeste* story. In the early hours of the morning of Tuesday, 12th January, 1897, the Norwegian brig Amarant loaded with oak, was seen drifting between the two piers of Redcar and Coatham. Warnings went unheeded. Several Redcar fishermen boarded her; they found the lights burning but no-one else aboard.

The Amarant had been abandoned during dense fog and had drifted at the mercy of the wind and tide until eventually coming ashore at Redcar. The crew of the abandoned vessel had been picked up by a passing steamer bound for the Tees. Having been deserted, the wreck became the property of the fishermen who brought her to the beach. No doubt the oak was put to many uses locally. A week later the Amarant was broken up in a storm and only her hull remained. The following day, the hull was driven by the storm through Redcar pier, making a breach in the pier eighty yards wide.

THE WRECK OF THE "BIRGER"

T HE barque Birger met a tragic fate on Saltscar rocks. Loaded with salt she had sprung a leak near the Dogger Bank, a hundred miles away. Flamborough Head was the nearest land, yet it took four days through gales to sight it. The furious seas prevented the barque making land. Word was sent along the storm lashed coast of the vessel's distress. Scarborough and Runswick Bay lifeboats were unable to assist. Whitby lifeboat was standing by but the waterlogged craft was driven three miles offshore as she passed the port. Word reached Redcar ahead of the Birger on 22nd October, 1898.

Several thousand people were gathered to witness the sad spectacle. Crashing over Saltscar, her masts snapped and both the captain and the chief officer were killed by the falling debris. The national lifeboat, The Brothers, was hauled down to the beach and rowed out through the mountainous seas. Dismasted, all that remained of the luckless vessel was the hull with the helpless crew clinging to it for their lives. Cheers went up from Coatham Pier as a piece of wreckage with three men clinging to it, was swept towards the pier. Ropes were lowered and as the makeshift raft passed under the pier one man was hauled to safety. A second clambered up then, nearing the top, fell back exhausted, to his death in the foaming sea. The third was washed away, then thrown by the sea on to the beach and revived. Only these two of the crew of fifteen lived. Had the vessel been able to run ashore, the Rocket Brigade could have saved the crew by firing lifelines from the shore, across the vessel. The wreck broke through Coatham pier, leaving a gap a hundred yards wide and came to rest on Coatham sands.

The following day, wreckage was strewn for miles along the beaches and as was their custom, many of the locals were there picking up anything that might be of value or use. The coastguards were unable to patrol the scattered wreckage and prevent the pilferage. A sad ending to a brave attempt to reach safety. Months later, a letter was received from Finland thanking the people of Redcar who had sent Christmas gifts to the bereaved families of the crew of the Birger.

THE AMALGAMATION

THE initiative for amalgamating the two boards came from Kirkleatham. The Redcar Local Board resolutely opposed the idea to the bitter end. In 1887, the Kirkleatham Board first brought the matter before the Local Government Board, claiming that they were acting in response to a petition which they had received.

The petition in favour of amalgamating the Boards was signed by a large number of the ratepayers of both districts. Redcar challenged the validity of the petition. They claimed that many of the signatures had been obtained under false pretences and that many who had signed the petition were now anxious to sign a petition opposing the move. The Redcar Board then passed a resolution opposing the motion, embodying the following points :

The majority of the property owners and large ratepayers were against the amalgamation.

Only two members of Redcar's Board were in favour.

The Earl of Zetland was against it.

The Board could see no advantage in such a change.

In 1894 there was a change in the formation of local government; Urban District Councils replaced the Local Boards of Health. That same year, Kirkleatham U.D.C. made a further application to the North Riding County Council. The new Redcar Council still considered the proposed change "neither desirable nor necessary." A committee was appointed to oppose any move to bring about amalgamation.

When the County Council reached its decision, it was certainly not to the liking of Kirkleatham U.D.C. In 1896, by order of the County Council, the parish of Kirkleatham was to be divided into two separate parishes. Coatham was to be amalgamated with Redcar; Kirkleatham, Yearby and Dunsdale were to revert to the control of Guisborough Rural Sanitary Authority. There was an outcry from all concerned. The right of appeal to the Local Government Board was promptly exercised. An inquiry was held at the Coatham Hotel on 21st April, 1897, and as a result, the original order was not confirmed. The following year, an amended order was made by the County Council. This too was resisted but it was becoming accepted that the amalgamation was inevitable. On Wednesday, 1st March, 1899, the communities of Redcar and Coatham were united under one Urban District Council. There were twelve councillors, six from each ward. The union of the rivals was further cemented when the continued growth of the town, early in the twentieth century, merited the transition to the status of Municipal Borough Council.

No public celebrations marked the turn of the century, yet the nineteenth century had probably been the most important in the history of Redcar and Coatham. Both had remained unchanged for a millenium, two quiet fishing villages, their existence barely noticed by the outside world. The nineteenth century had brought social and industrial changes undreamt of. Both communities had come of age and been well and truly wedded.

Bibliography

The History of Cleveland, 1808, John Graves

A Trip to Coatham, 1810, W. Hutton

The History and Antiquities of Cleveland, 1846, John Walker Ord

The Visitors' Guide to Redcar, 1841, John Walbran

The Visitors' Guide to Redcar, 1848, John Walbran

History of Cleveland, Ancient and Modern, Vol. 2, J. C. Atkinson

Visitors' Handbook to Redcar, Coatham and Saltburn-by-Sea, 1863, Tweddell

The Local Records of Stockton and the Neighbourhood, Thomas Richmond

A Short History of Redcar Racecourse, J. Fairfax Blakeborough

Railways in Cleveland, K. Hoole

North Eastern Railway, Wm. Weaver Tomlinson

Rambles Through Redcar, Saltburn and Neighbourhood, 1888, Angus Macpherson

Shipwrecks of the Yorkshire Coast, A. Godfrey & P. J. Lassey

Redcar in Retrospect, Peter Sotheran

The History of Marske-by-Sea, Edmund Hope

The Turners of Kirkleatham and Their Descendents, Arthur Baldwin

Directories and Gazetteers

Langdale, Thomas, *A Topographical Dictionary of Yorkshire,* 2nd ed., 1822

Baines, Edward, *History, Directory and Gazetteer of the County of Yorkshire,* Vol. 2, 1823

White, William, *History, Gazetteer and Directory of the East and North Ridings of Yorkshire,* 1840

Slater's, *Royal National Commercial Directory of the Counties of Cumberland, Durham, Northumberland, Westmorland and the Cleveland District,* 1876-1877

Bulmer, T., *History, Topography and Directory of North Yorkshire,* 1890

Kelly's Directory of the North and East Ridings of Yorkshire, 1893

Old Newspapers

Yorkshire Gazette
The Evening Gazette
Middlesbrough News and Cleveland Advertiser
Daily Exchange
Weekly Exchange
Redcar and Saltburn News
Redcar and Saltburn Gazette

Maps and Plans

Ordnance Survey Maps, 1851 and 1895
Plan of Redcar, 1815 (from Zetland Collection)
Peat's Plan of Redcar, 1861

Census Returns

Redcar, 1851 and 1871
Coatham, 1851 and 1871

Council Records

Redcar Local Board of Health Minutes, 1860-1894
Redcar Urban District Council Minutes, 1894-1899
Kirkleatham Local Board of Health Minutes, 1877-1894
Kirkleatham Urban District Council Minutes, 1894-1899
Redcar (and Coatham) Urban District Council Minutes, 1899-1901

School Records

Zetland School Log Books, 1863-1901

Sanitary Reports

*Superintending Inspector's Report to the General Board of Health
on the Sanitary Condition of Redcar* 1855
A Special Report on the Sanitary Condition of Redcar
*A Special Report on the Sanitary Conditions of Kirkleatham
District with Reference to the State of Preparedness to With-
stand any Invasion of Cholera*
Report by Dr. Barry on Enteric Fever in Tees Valley Towns

Miscellaneous

Prospectus of the Redcar Railway

Proposed Asylum Harbour and Naval Station at Redcar on the Coast of Yorkshire . . . to be Called Port William, 1834. W. A. Brookes

Redcar and Coatham Literary Institute Exhibition News, 1901, 1901-2, 1903

Memorial . . . of an Indenture Bearing the date 10th May, 1862 Between Teresa Newcomen and Rev. John Postlethwaite . . . Concerning Coatham Common

Declaration of Trust in Respect of the Coatham Convalescent Home and Children's Hospital dated 25th April, 1893. Mary Postlethwaite and others

The Cleveland and Teesside Local History Session Bulletin II, Dec., 1970

The Port of Coatham, 1789 to 1808, D. W. Pattenden

A Parting Word or Redcar as it is and Redcar as it should be, Unknown Writer, 1864